FOR THE LOVE OF KEWPIE

KEWPIE CORPORATION

Text
ELYSE INAMINE

Recipes
JESSIE YUCHEN

Photographs
HEAMI LEE

Creative direction and Food Styling
EUGENE JHO

for the love of kewpie

A COOKBOOK and CELEBRATION

WORKMAN PUBLISHING
NEW YORK

Copyright © 2025 Kewpie Corporation
Photography copyright © 2025 Heami Lee, except on page 95: © CBC TELEVISION; pages 4-5, 7, 9, 11, 22-23, 34-35, 45, 50-51, 56-57, 61, 69, 74-75, 82-83, 96-97, 104-107, 114-115, 125-126, 128, 148-149, 155, 160-161: Kewpie Corporation

Hachette Book Group supports the right to free expression and the value of copyright. The purpose of copyright is to encourage writers and artists to produce the creative works that enrich our culture.

The scanning, uploading, and distribution of this book without permission is a theft of the author's intellectual property. If you would like permission to use material from the book (other than for review purposes), please contact permissions@hbgusa.com. Thank you for your support of the author's rights.

Workman
Workman Publishing
Hachette Book Group, Inc.
1290 Avenue of the Americas
New York, NY 10104
workman.com

Workman is an imprint of Workman Publishing, a division of Hachette Book Group, Inc. The Workman name and logo are registered trademarks of Hachette Book Group, Inc.

Design by Jack Dunnington
Prop Styling by Julia Rose

The publisher is not responsible for websites (or their content) that are not owned by the publisher.

The Hachette Speakers Bureau provides a wide range of authors for speaking events. To find out more, go to hachettespeakersbureau.com or email HachetteSpeakers@hbgusa.com.

Workman books may be purchased in bulk for business, educational, or promotional use. For information, please contact your local bookseller or the Hachette Book Group Special Markets Department at special.markets@hbgusa.com.

Library of Congress Cataloging-in-Publication Data is available.
ISBN 978-1-5235-3300-8
First Edition October 2025
Printed in China APO on responsibly sourced paper.

10 9 8 7 6 5 4 3 2 1

目次

contents

Foreword

1

———

SIDES
and
SALADS

46

———

DESSERTS

144

Introduction

2

SNACKS

16

RICE *and* **NOODLES**

76

MEAT, SEAFOOD, *and* TOFU

112

Index

162

Acknowledgments

166

FOREWORD
CHEF MASAHARU MORIMOTO

Kewpie Mayonnaise is common in most households in Japan. Growing up there, I often saw the Japanese condiment being whisked into eggs for a creamier scramble and spread onto grilled cheese sandwiches instead of butter. However, it wasn't until I was older and starting my career as a chef that I began to take note of Kewpie.

From my earliest days as a young chef in Hiroshima, where I first learned to pair delicate Japanese flavors with Western cuisine, to high-energy kitchens around the world, I have always carried with me an appreciation for ingredients that embody simplicity and depth. Kewpie Mayonnaise is one of these ingredients. Its unique taste—a perfect blend of richness and tanginess—introduced me to the complex art of balancing flavor, and in turn, influenced my approach to cooking. Each ingredient in a dish must harmonize with the others to create a symphony of flavors on the plate. Kewpie, with its creamy texture and distinctive umami, played an important role in teaching me this lesson.

As we commemorate one hundred years of Kewpie Mayonnaise, I am reminded of the impact this iconic condiment has had not only on my personal culinary journey but on Japanese cuisine as well. Rooted in careful ingredient selection, precise culinary techniques, and a harmonious blending of tradition with innovation, Japanese cooking finds a true representative in Kewpie Mayonnaise.

Since its inception in 1925, the recipe for this cherished condiment has been thoughtfully refined, staying true to its origins while embracing contemporary tastes. This makes Kewpie Mayonnaise a versatile and timeless addition to traditional Japanese dishes and beyond. From enhancing okonomiyaki to giving decadent chocolate cake a fluffy texture, Kewpie serves as a bridge. This book pays respect to an ingredient that has shaped the landscape of not only Japanese cuisine but also global cuisine.

As you turn the pages of this book, I invite you to explore, experiment, and experience the charm of Kewpie Mayonnaise. Whether you are a home cook or a professional chef, the story of Kewpie and the versatility of its power in the kitchen will inspire new ideas and deepen your appreciation for what a simple yet exceptional ingredient can do. Remember: Cooking is not just about following recipes; it's about making each ingredient shine—and Kewpie Mayonnaise does that beautifully.

Thank you for joining us in this celebration, and may you find as much joy in these recipes as I have found in the journey of culinary exploration that Kewpie has afforded me.

INTRODUCTION

WELCOME to the WORLD of KEWPIE MAYONNAISE

There is only one mayonnaise that's luxuriously creamy yet light as a cloud and *extremely* savory. It's zigzagged and drizzled onto dishes with unabashed abandon, as satisfying to squeeze as it is to devour. This is a condiment with a cult following and the most adorable logo, and it's probably already in your fridge: Kewpie Mayonnaise.

The Japanese mayo is a pulls-no-punches version of the American condiment with a deep richness, tangy zip, and undercurrent of umami. While many home cooks have experienced the joy of adding Kewpie Mayonnaise to whatever they're eating, most don't know how this powerhouse of an ingredient came to be. Its origin story has been speculated on by many but never told in its strange and delightful entirety—until now.

THE START OF KEWPIE'S STORY

No one remembers the first time they tasted mayonnaise. In the symphony of a well-composed dish, mayonnaise is the background noise of ingredients: a perfunctory smear on a sandwich, an ambivalent companion to chunky salads (potato, egg, chicken), a nice addition to any dish but never the main attraction. No one bites into a BLT and excitedly exclaims, "Wow, the mayo!"

There was, however, one person who distinctly recalled his first encounter with mayonnaise. His name was Toichiro Nakashima—and the experience changed not only his life but that of home cooks worldwide.

In the early 1900s, Nakashima began his career in the seafood canning business, then a budding industry in Japan, and traveled to the United Kingdom and the United States as a business intern to further his understanding of the trade. Or at least that was the plan. Somewhere in the United States, sometime during World War I, Nakashima was invited to a meal hosted by a canned seafood manufacturer. He enjoyed course after course, but one dish captivated him: canned salmon punctuated with finely chopped onion and finished with mayonnaise.

Lore has it that he loved the "new, dainty food." Later, he stumbled upon potato salad and found its mayonnaise-lathered composition "delicious, affordable, and nutritious." Nakashima noticed how the condiment was so entwined with American food, and in turn, how strong and healthy these Americans were. Upon returning to Japan, he knew he wanted to make mayonnaise—in Japan and for Japanese people.

The man behind the mayonnaise, Toichiro Nakashima, painted by Japanese artist Usaburo Ihara

In 1925, Nakashima launched the first mayonnaise ever made in Japan: Kewpie Mayonnaise. His version was unlike any other in the world. It was rich from egg yolks (as opposed to whole eggs) and came in a glass jar with the illustrated Kewpie character on the label. At first, some early customers confused the mayonnaise for hair oil, but soon enough, Kewpie Mayonnaise became a staple in Japanese home kitchens.

Nakashima had a lofty goal, believing that Kewpie could "improve the physiques and health of Japanese people by making delicious, nutritious mayonnaise widely available so that it would become a daily necessity." But he had no idea just how successful he'd be. Today, Kewpie Mayonnaise is not only Japan's most popular mayonnaise; it's also a global condiment, sold in thousands upon thousands of grocery stores in more than seventy countries and regions, and a welcome addition to any and every dish, from katsu sando to spaghetti and meatballs.

Even in this day and age, there still is nothing like Kewpie Mayonnaise. Made with just a few ingredients—a blend of oil and vinegar, egg yolks, MSG, salt, and some secret flavorings—this mayo isn't a wallflower but a flavor-packed condiment that makes an impression. Kewpie has been hailed as "the clear winner" by the *Chicago Tribune* in a blind taste test of mayos and the "one store-bought mayo that nearly every professional chef

印マヨネーズに就て

一、欧米に於て用ひらる、各種調味品の中で一番日本人の嗜好に適して居るのはマヨネーズ（一名サラダドレッシング）で有ると思ひます

二、キユーピー印マヨネーズは新鮮な鶏卵の黄身と純良なる植物油とから出来て居りますから美味で有るばかりでなく又極めて滋養分に富だ物で有ります

三、それ故近来其の需要が著るしく増へて参りました。然かし只今の處始んど全部米國若しくは英國からの輸入品で有ります

四、將來盆々需要の増進すべき商品を全部外国からの輸入に仰ぐとは誠に不面目なる事と考へられますので其共に不快業に従事して居る私共は誠に不面目の事と考へ今より一ケ年前から種々研究を重ねました結果漸く今日のキユーピー印マヨネーズを造り得る様になりました

五、従来舶来品を内地で製造する場合には「値段は少しも安いが品物がをとる」と云ふのが殆んど免れ難い缺點で有りました

したが今回發賣のキユーピー印マヨネーズは
「値段は舶来品よりも低廉に」
「品質は舶来品よりも優良に」と云ふ目標に充分到達したものと確信して居ります

六、目下日本へ輸入されて居りますマヨネーズは凡そ七八種類有りますから共何れとでも御比較の上果してキユーピー印マヨネーズの風味が他より優れて居りましたら微かな私共の苦心を御認め下さいまして是非御知り合ひの方々に御吹聽を御願ひ致し度いので有ります

用ひ方
エビサラダ、カニサラダ、鮭サラダ、ハムサラダ、トマト、アスパラガス、サンドヰッチ、焼魚、照焼魚など、牛豚肉、魚、野菜類にかけますと簡單で精構なお料理が出来ます

製造元 食品工業株式會社
東京中野

This early product description touted that Kewpie Mayonnaise is made with "fresh egg yolks and pure vegetable oils."

and in-the-know food lover keeps in their chill chest," according to *Food & Wine*. Case in point: David Chang of the Momofuku empire declared Kewpie "the best mayonnaise in the world."

Now, a century after its invention, Kewpie Mayonnaise has taken over the world. It's regularly stocked at supermarkets (sometimes selling out due to its popularity on social media platforms) and universally coveted among food lovers, particularly the serious mayonnaise fans known as mayolers (page 149). Kewpie has shed those old glass jars for packaging that has become iconic in its own right: a supple, squeezable, bowling pin–shaped bottle with a signature tomato-red cap and, of course, the Kewpie character.

In 1982, Kewpie made a giant leap for mayo kind and began manufacturing its Japanese mayonnaise where the very idea originated for Nakashima, the United States. (Though how it first got to America is a bit of an accident; see page 3.) The company started off small, with just an old 710-square-foot warehouse it turned into a mayonnaise factory and office and from which it supplied Japanese restaurants in America. The story of Kewpie came full circle in 2016 when Kewpie launched the American-made, Japanese-style mayonnaise directly to home cooks in the U.S.

ABOUT THIS BOOK

One hundred years after the debut of Kewpie Mayonnaise, this book celebrates the story of the mayonnaise that continually inspires.

Kewpie Mayonnaise is more than just an ordinary pantry item. It's one young man's dream of nourishing his people. It's a powerful ingredient that makes whatever it's squeezed into better, from creamy mashed potatoes to fish tacos. It's magnetic, pulling choirs of singing mothers, chefs, and more into its expansive and eclectic orbit of fans. It's a condiment the world has fallen for, unlocking creativity for some cooks and providing comforting familiarity for others.

In these pages, you'll meet Toichiro Nakashima, Kewpie's founder, who was constantly confounded by how to use up all those extra egg whites (page 34). Learn about the early days of Kewpie Mayonnaise, including the original bottle designs and the company's specially made egg-cracking machines (handling 600 eggs at a time!). You'll get a taste of what makes Kewpie Mayonnaise so different from other mayos and how to wring out every last bit left in the bottle (page 64). You'll meet some Kewpie employees, too—they're nice.

The fifty recipes in this book harness the full power of Kewpie beyond the expected drizzle of the condiment. Kewpie is the secret ingredient to the flakiest apple galette (page 158) and fall-apart-tender baby back ribs with hot honey (page 143), and the key to easily emulsifying carbonara (page 102). And of course, you'll find the ultimate recipe for tamago sando, the elite Japanese egg salad sandwich (page 116). Kewpie Mayonnaise is also the most versatile substitution in so many cooking applications—frying, baking, stir-frying—whether that's to make crispy fritto misto (page 135), lemon cupcakes (page 156), or classic yakisoba (page 101).

No matter how you spread or squiggle or dot it, consider this your invitation to the world of Kewpie Mayonnaise.

A NOTE ON SOURCING KEWPIE

You may have noticed that Kewpie Mayonnaise has tiny variations depending on where you buy it. Generally speaking, the American-made mayonnaise has slightly different formulations than the mayonnaise from Japan that contains MSG. While some Kewpie fans swear by one bottle over the other, all Kewpie Mayonnaise is Kewpie Mayonnaise. So no matter which one you purchase, you're getting the yolk-rich, flavor-forward goodness of Kewpie—meaning there is no wrong choice. Feel free to explore the bottles you see on your grocery store shelves and online to see which is best for you. Happy squeezing!

WHY THE KEWPIE CHARACTER?

Kewpie didn't invent this cherubic being; rather, it was the design of Rose O'Neill, an American artist. She first created Kewpie for the December 1909 issue of *Ladies' Home Journal*, thinking of the character as "a benevolent elf who did good deeds in a funny way." Kewpies appeared in newspaper cartoons and soon after were manufactured and sold as dolls that sparked international demand, including in Japan. Toichiro Nakashima noticed how Kewpie captivated Japanese people, and at the nudging of his mentor, he sought to make it part of his brand. In 1922, he procured the Japanese trademark to the Kewpie name and character. Nakashima's reasoning was simple: Kewpie dolls were popular and beloved by consumers, and he wanted his mayonnaise to also be popular and beloved by consumers. Three years after securing the trademark, he introduced Kewpie Mayonnaise. It came in a small glass jar with a blue-and-red label that featured an image of the Kewpie with its pudgy arms open wide.

The Inimitable
TOICHIRO NAKASHIMA

The spirit of Kewpie's founder is best captured in a speech he gave in 1966 after receiving the Manager of the Year award from *Zaikai*, a reputable Japanese business magazine. Nakashima's remarks were short: "Mayonnaise is a simple product that can be made easily at home as long as good materials are used. Being a manufacturer of such a simple thing, we have been honored with this esteemed commendation. This is truly a great encouragement to me and those working with me. With this, we will refresh our commitment to delivering good food products to help improve the health and physique of Japanese people."

After the award ceremony, other attendees left in fancy foreign cars while he hopped in a company van.

Nakashima was quirky from the start. Born in 1883 in modern-day Nishio in the Aichi prefecture of Japan, he decided to study seafood canning, then a nascent industry, simply because he enjoyed swimming and boating. He later applied for an overseas business internship with Japan's Ministry of Agriculture and Commerce, and while Nakashima picked up industry-specific insight during his travels, the most significant moment of his three-year trip was discovering mayonnaise in the United States (and orange marmalade in the UK). (Read about his first taste of mayonnaise on page 3.) Both became his white whales, the "subjects of my lifelong business pursuit," he later reflected.

Nakashima succeeded in realizing these condiment dreams, crafting and selling Kewpie Mayonnaise in 1925 (and Aohata orange marmalade in 1932). This wasn't an easy feat. Nakashima was navigating unknown waters, establishing both his own company's process for making mayonnaise and industry standards for the growing market—all while consumer trends and the world at large fluctuated.

Nakashima mid-speech at the Manager of the Year award ceremony

    The company stopped manufacturing mayonnaise during World War II, but after it ended, Nakashima refused to bend to industry norms (and employee pressure) to procure hard-to-find ingredients from the black market. He held his ground—and held off on production. Once work resumed in 1948, he personally inspected key ingredients and even started a vinegar company to better complement the mayonnaise. Later, he found time to write letters to the parents of his employees, assuring them their children were in good care, a tradition the sitting Kewpie chairman carries on to this day.

    Nakashima led Kewpie Corporation for fifty-four years, until his death in 1973. The company maintains strong ties to its founding family, with the third generation of Nakashimas now involved in the business. Today, his legacy lives on: Nakashima not only introduced an entire country to a very American condiment, but also established it as a distinctly Japanese one.

The FOUNDER'S COMMANDMENTS

Following are some of Nakashima's most interesting (and insightful) thoughts on business, duty, and of course, mayonnaise.

1
"The world is fairer than you imagine."

As a young man, Nakashima read this phrase in a publication, and it inspired him to work with integrity and ingenuity, even in difficult or unjust circumstances. This saying became a constant refrain in his life, and eventually, a principle of Kewpie Corporation.

2
"You may face many problems, slow progress, and financial deficits. However, once you've decided, never give up until you succeed."

Nakashima to his colleague who wanted to get into the baby food business in the 1950s. The statement reflects his belief in careful consideration and unwavering commitment once a path is chosen.

3
"I prefer to not make a large company."

Nakashima to a new board member in the late 1940s, revealing his desire to build a company of like-minded colleagues over big profits.

4
"What is right is right, no matter who says it. So listen to anyone if you think what they say is right."

This is how Nakashima advised Kewpie management when one manufacturing plant unionized in 1962, a surprising take for an executive even today and telling of his personal morals.

5

"A factory we take pride in is not one that is simply large or has high-performance machinery but it is where the people come to have a common goal and cooperate with each other."

While Nakashima always invested in new technology and equipment, he wrote this in a memo in 1956 to emphasize his focus on people and collaboration.

6

"The primary thing we must aspire to do right away is first respect moral principles rather than pursue profits."

Nakashima welcomed all new employees with a letter, which included this declaration to ensure new hires understood Kewpie's culture.

7

"One of the most valuable things in the world is parents' love for their children. I ask all employees to practice filial piety."

Nakashima emphasized this idea, teaching that filial piety extends beyond parents to appreciating and repaying kindness from all. It remains a company principle.

8

"Mayonnaise is a simple product that can be made easily at home as long as good materials are used."

Upon winning a business leadership award in 1966, Nakashima opened his acceptance speech with this line, humbly assessing his product and his continued commitment to making high-quality mayo.

WHAT EXACTLY *is* KEWPIE MAYO?

Over the last one hundred years, Kewpie's formulation has been refined to its present-day perfection. There are certain things that have always been essential to the recipe, whereas other elements have been adapted over the years.

There are lots of theories about Kewpie's formulation—and attempts at homemade versions—swirling around in the zeitgeist. But here's the truth about what goes into a bottle of Kewpie Mayonnaise.

OIL

All mayonnaise is primarily made from oil, and Kewpie is no exception. A large portion of the condiment is vegetable oil, using a blend of canola and soybean oils. Initially, like many Japanese mayonnaise manufacturers in the 1940s, Kewpie relied on imported oils, though Nakashima sought to improve the quality of domestic oil. He built cooperative relationships within the Japanese oil industry, gradually refining the sourcing of raw materials and manufacturing techniques over time. Today, Kewpie uses premium vegetable oils from Japanese producers that are carefully selected, and this commitment to quality is largely due to Nakashima's perseverance.

EGG YOLKS

Emphasis on "yolks." This is what sets Kewpie Mayonnaise apart. Most American-style mayos rely on whole eggs, but Kewpie scoops out just the sunny yolks for its recipe. There are about four egg yolks in each 450-gram bottle of Kewpie Mayonnaise, and they're crucial to its intense, almost butter-like richness and cream-colored hue. In the early days, the company started Nishifu Farm to make sure it had enough high-quality eggs for mayonnaise production. Since then, Kewpie has continued to double down on egg production, using millions (millions!) of eggs each year to make Kewpie Mayonnaise.

SALT, SPICE & NATURAL FLAVORS

?

Sorry, our lips are sealed on this one. Kewpie keeps the lineup of seasonings close to the vest, but some die-hard Kewpie fans say they detect garlic powder and mustard powder. You'll have to try for yourself!

VINEGAR

The unsung hero of Kewpie Mayonnaise, this ingredient is responsible for the condiment's mellow tang. It's a mixture of vinegars brewed from apple juice and malt, the final blend being the product of a *lot* of tinkering. When Kewpie began making mayonnaise, Nakashima couldn't find any Western-style vinegars in Japan that were up to his standards. He ended up collaborating with Japanese breweries to produce vinegar out of sake lees and rice. In 1962, he established what is now Kewpie Jyozo Co. to create his own Western-style vinegar that has the right balance of sour perkiness and round sweetness.

MSG

Also known as monosodium glutamate, this flavorful compound is responsible for the distinctly savory, borderline nutty taste that's naturally occurring in tomatoes and Parmesan. In America MSG can be a divisive ingredient, but in Japan it's part of daily life. Japanese biochemist Kikunae Ikeda discovered it in 1908 when trying to figure out what made kombu, Japanese kelp, just so savory. The exact amount sprinkled into Kewpie Mayonnaise is top secret, but it's essential to the mayo's signature umami-loaded taste.

ANATOMY of the KEWPIE BOTTLE

Every little detail that makes it so iconic and useful

Kewpie Mayonnaise came in glass jars when it first hit the shelves in 1925, and in 1958, the now-familiar soft, teardrop-shaped squeezable bottles were adopted. Today, Kewpie's minimal yet striking package has become design canon in the condiment world. The bottle has been the subject of research among packaging experts in Japan, one going so far as to say the bottle embodies classic Japanese aesthetic, with its simple form and whitish color.

Good looks aside, the function of these bottles is equally important and influential in why Kewpie looks the way it looks. Here's the how and why behind the bottle.

❶ The bottle: Funnily enough, how the Kewpie bottle got its distinctive shape is a mystery to all. While the source of the idea has been lost to history, the design was introduced in 1958. Today, the bottle is made with multiple layers of polyethylene and EVOH (ethylene vinyl alcohol), which keep out oxygen better than the original glass jars, resulting in a fresher mayo. Still, Kewpie constantly tweaks the design. For example, for Kewpie Mayonnaise manufactured in the United States, the company switched to bottles made from recycled PET (polyethylene terephthalate) in 2023.

❷ The cap: A cap may seem like no big deal, but it's an important part of what makes Kewpie special. Kewpie's cap has an extended nozzle for precise squiggling, and the hinges have been minimized and strengthened so that your fingers don't bump into them (and to protect the top from snapping off). Unique to Kewpie's cap are two tips: One is a thin nozzle built into the cap and the second is a star-shaped opening cut into the top of the bottle itself. Make the most of these tips on page 60.

❸ The plastic bag: The bottle-in-a-bag phenomenon is a common packaging practice in Japan, and on Kewpie's bag, you'll find the product information and company logo. The color red is used here for its bold flair but also because it has been said to stimulate the appetite. As for the mesh pattern, it's inspired by tablecloths in Western-style restaurants.

❹ The Kewpie character: Though the fairy on the bottle has become a beloved symbol of Kewpie, the character actually originated in America in 1909 (see page 7). The cartoon charmed founder Toichiro Nakashima so much that he made it the face of Kewpie Mayonnaise.

❺ The secret label: Once the whole bottle is used up, a little surprise awaits: a hidden Kewpie character. At the center of the bottle is a clear embossed logo that adds a nice textural feel to the bottle before you even notice it.

スナック

snacks

TAMAGOYAKI 19

DEVILED EGGS 20

CRUDITÉ AND RANCH 24

CORN DIP 27

PIMENTO CHEESE DIP 28

SMOKED FISH DIP 31

SOY-GLAZED CHICKEN WINGS 37

POTATO TAKOYAKI 38

OVEN-FRIED SHRIMP 41

SEAWEED FRIES 42

BUFFALO CAULIFLOWER BITES 44

Tamagoyaki

This soft Japanese-style rolled omelet is traditionally made with a special tamagoyaki pan, but a nonstick skillet and a little patience as you slowly roll the thin layers of quick-cooking egg will do the trick. What makes this particular tamagoyaki extra fluffy, even after it cools, is the addition of Kewpie. The oil and vinegar in the mayo break down any stringy bits of egg. Serve the tamagoyaki sliced as part of a bento box, on its own as a protein-rich side to accompany a meal, or stacked in a sandwich—with an extra swipe of Kewpie Mayonnaise, of course.

SERVES 2

6 large eggs

1 tablespoon mirin

1 teaspoon Kewpie Mayonnaise, plus more for serving

½ teaspoon kosher salt

½ teaspoon hondashi (dashi powder)

½ teaspoon toasted sesame oil

Cooking spray or 1 teaspoon neutral vegetable oil, such as canola

Furikake, for serving

1. In a medium bowl, whisk the eggs, mirin, mayonnaise, salt, hondashi, and sesame oil until fully combined and no streaks of egg white remain.

2. Pour the egg mixture through a fine-mesh strainer into another bowl, swirling the strainer occasionally to help the liquid pass through. Discard any solids left in the strainer.

3. Place a tamagoyaki pan or medium nonstick pan over medium-low heat. Coat the pan with a thin layer of cooking spray.

4. Pour about 3 tablespoons (45 ml) of the egg mixture into the pan. Tilt the pan quickly to spread the egg evenly across the surface. Cook until the egg is mostly set but still slightly moist, about 3 to 4 minutes.

5. Starting from the far edge of the pan, use chopsticks or two flexible spatulas to roll the egg toward you. Once rolled, slide the omelet to the far edge of the pan.

6. Pour another thin layer of the egg mixture into the pan, lifting the rolled omelet slightly to let the new mixture flow underneath. Cook and roll as before. Repeat until all the egg mixture is used.

7. Transfer the rolled omelet, seam side down, to a cutting board and let cool for 5 minutes. Slice crosswise into ½-inch (1.25 cm) or 1-inch-wide (2 cm) pieces.

8. Top with a drizzle of mayonnaise and a sprinkle of furikake and serve immediately. Leftovers will keep in an airtight container in the refrigerator for up to 3 days.

Deviled Eggs

Is there a more decadent deviled egg than one that is topped with *more* eggs? And by "more eggs," we mean salty, punchy salmon roe. This recipe is inspired by Japanese flavors: The egg yolks are mixed with shichimi togarashi (a seven-spice blend) for a little heat and Kewpie Mayonnaise for a velvety texture and a hit of seaweed-like savoriness. Each half is crowned with a few pearls of salmon roe, which you can find fresh or frozen at Asian grocery stores. If frozen, all you need to do is thaw the roe overnight in the fridge, and then you're ready for deviling.

MAKES 12 DEVILED EGGS

6 large hard-boiled eggs

1/3 cup (80 ml) Kewpie Mayonnaise

1 teaspoon Dijon mustard

1/2 teaspoon shichimi togarashi (seven-spice blend), plus more for serving

1/4 teaspoon honey

1/2 teaspoon white pepper, plus more as needed

1/4 teaspoon kosher salt, plus more as needed

Salmon roe, for serving

Thinly sliced fresh chives, for serving

1. Peel and slice the eggs in half lengthwise. Use a small spoon to carefully scoop the egg yolks out into a medium bowl. Arrange the egg whites, cut side up, on a large plate or serving platter.

2. Mash the egg yolks with a fork or spoon until finely crumbled, with no chunks remaining. Add the mayonnaise, Dijon mustard, shichimi togarashi, honey, white pepper, and salt. Stir everything together with a spoon until the mixture is smooth and uniform. Add salt or white pepper as needed.

3. Use a small spoon to carefully fill the egg whites with the yolk mixture. For a more decorative presentation, fill a piping bag with the yolk mixture, cutting a ½-inch (1.25 cm) opening at the tip, and pipe into the egg whites.

4. Garnish each egg with a small amount of salmon roe, a sprinkle of shichimi togarashi, and a few slices of chives. Serve right away.

Kewpie by the Decade: The 1920s

Fresh from a few years abroad in the UK and the United States, where he first discovered mayonnaise, Toichiro Nakashima started Shokuhin Kogyo Co. in Tokyo in 1919.

Nakashima began manufacturing sauces with middling success. But on September 1, 1923, everything changed. Just before noon that day, a 7.9 magnitude earthquake hit Japan, devastating Tokyo and nearby prefectures. Nakashima watched as the country rebuilt itself while Westernizing at the same time; for Japanese urban planners, this was an opportunity to adopt Western infrastructure such as skyscrapers. Nakashima had an inkling this influence would spread beyond construction. He saw how female students traded their traditional hakama for European sailor-style uniforms, and he imagined Japanese home cooks would reach for Western pantry ingredients, perhaps even mayonnaise.

In 1925, Nakashima debuted Kewpie Mayonnaise, the first mayonnaise produced in Japan. He painstakingly recreated his own version of the American condiment he had fallen in love with when he visited the United States as a business intern a decade earlier. (Read about this life-changing trip on page 3.) Kewpie Mayonnaise only used egg yolks (as opposed to whole eggs, common in ready-made mayonnaise at the time and even now), resulting in a richer flavor, and adopted the iconic Kewpie character for the label design.

It was a risky bet. At this point, the country wasn't familiar with the American condiment—some customers even confused it for hair oil. Shokuhin Kogyo Co. employees visited grocers to convince them to stock the mayonnaise, mixing it with canned seafood for them to try, just as Nakashima had enjoyed it in America.

In its first year, just 120 cases of Kewpie Mayonnaise were sold. But the next year, that number jumped to 1,000 cases. Nakashima was onto something.

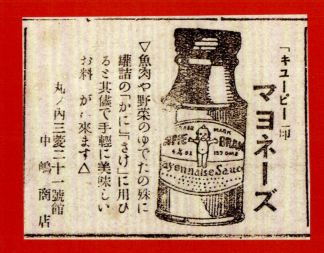

This 1926 ad recommends Kewpie Mayonnaise with salmon, the same way Nakashima first tried it.

KEWPIE COMES TO LIFE

Batches of Kewpie Mayonnaise initially came in glass bottles like this.

Crudité and Ranch

Classic ranch dressing is usually made with buttermilk, but this version subs in Kewpie Mayonnaise, which provides not only a vinegary sweet punch but also an umami undertone. It's easy to throw together—just whisk the mayo with sour cream and lemon juice—but much better than the bottled stuff, since it has fresh herbs that you can actually taste. You might want to double up on the dressing; it keeps in the fridge for up to 3 days.

MAKES 1 CUP

- ½ cup (120 ml) Kewpie Mayonnaise
- ½ cup (120 ml) sour cream
- 1 tablespoon chopped fresh dill
- 1 teaspoon finely chopped fresh parsley
- 1 tablespoon grated garlic
- ¼ teaspoon kosher salt, plus more as needed
- ¼ teaspoon freshly ground black pepper
- 1 teaspoon lemon juice, plus more as needed
- Assorted seasonal vegetables, such as cucumbers, radishes, and endives, for serving

1. In a medium bowl, whisk together the mayonnaise and sour cream until smooth. Add the dill, parsley, garlic, salt, and black pepper, and stir until combined. Add the lemon juice and whisk again. Season with salt and lemon juice as needed. Pour into a jar and chill in the refrigerator until ready to eat.
2. Serve with assorted vegetables.

★ A DISH POWERED BY KEWPIE ★

American troops introduced South Koreans to mayonnaise during the Korean War, and that led to a must-have side: corn cheese. For these kernels broiled in mozzarella and mayo, home cooks and chefs stick to one mayonnaise brand—ahem, Kewpie. It's savory and tangy, so when it caramelizes, those flavors intensify to complement the sugary corn. Regular mayo could never.

Corn Dip

This recipe is a riff on corn cheese, the iconic side dish at Korean barbecues and drinking dens. It has the usual oozy suspects—mozzarella and Kewpie Mayonnaise, which adds a milky sweetness—as well as a couple of outliers. The addition of freshly ground white pepper and chopped garlic imparts a sharp, slightly herbal savoriness that balances everything out. Eat this dip alongside a marinated meat feast, or serve with thick, buttery crackers as a party appetizer. Just move fast—it'll disappear before the dip gets cold.

SERVES 6

- 4 medium scallions, thinly sliced
- 16 ounces (455 g) coarsley grated low-moisture mozzarella
- 1 cup (240 ml) Kewpie Mayonnaise
- 1 teaspoon honey
- ¼ teaspoon kosher salt
- ½ teaspoon freshly ground white pepper
- 2 tablespoons chopped garlic
- Two 15-ounce (425 g) cans corn kernels, drained, or 3½ cups (596 g) fresh/frozen (thawed and drained) corn
- Thick, buttery-tasting crackers, such as Ritz, for serving

1. Arrange a rack about 6 inches (15 cm) from the broiler, then preheat the oven to 425°F (220°C).

2. Reserve about 2 tablespoons of the dark green parts of the scallions for serving, then add the remaining scallions to a large bowl. Add the mozzarella, mayonnaise, honey, salt, white pepper, and garlic to the bowl and stir to combine.

3. Add the corn to the bowl and stir to combine. Transfer the mixture to a 9-by-13-inch (23-by-33 cm) baking dish (or a 10-inch/25 cm cast-iron skillet). Spread into an even layer and smooth the top.

4. Bake until lightly browned and bubbling, 10 to 12 minutes. Switch the oven to broil and broil until the top is darker brown in spots, 2 to 4 minutes. Sprinkle with the reserved scallion greens and serve with crackers.

Pimento Cheese Dip

Lovingly referred to as the pâté of the South, this dip is the definition of a crowd pleaser. It's velvety thanks to the cream cheese, salty and nutty due to extra-sharp Cheddar, and spicy from pimento peppers. But what really gives this dish a certain je ne sais quoi is the Kewpie Mayonnaise. Mayonnaise is often used as a binder in pimento cheese, but Kewpie works double duty in this recipe by also giving the dip an intense savoriness. You can make this pimento cheese ahead of time, and it's great for loading onto crunchy vegetable sticks, crackers, and even a sandwich.

MAKES 2 CUPS

2 cups (170 g) grated extra-sharp Cheddar

8 ounces (225 g) cream cheese, cut into 1-inch (2.5 cm) cubes and softened at room temperature

4 ounces (115 g) well drained and thinly chopped jarred pimento peppers

2 tablespoons Kewpie Mayonnaise

½ teaspoon garlic powder

¼ teaspoon cayenne pepper

1 tablespoon minced jalapeño pepper, ribs and seeds removed

½ teaspoon freshly ground black pepper

Kosher salt, as needed

Celery sticks, bell pepper strips, or chips, for serving

1. In a large mixing bowl, combine the Cheddar, cream cheese, pimento peppers, mayonnaise, garlic powder, cayenne pepper, jalapeño, and black pepper.

2. Beat the mixture together with a sturdy wooden spoon or spatula until thoroughly combined.

3. Season with salt as needed and transfer the mixture to a serving bowl. Enjoy immediately with celery sticks, bell pepper strips, or chips.

4. The pimento cheese dip will keep in the refrigerator in an airtight container for up to a week. Allow the dip to soften up at room temperature for about 30 minutes before you plan to serve it.

Smoked Fish Dip

Few dips are as versatile as this one. It can anchor a party spread of snacks, hold guests over before a dinner party without filling them up, and make for one easy sandwich when spread between soft potato buns and crisp sliced cucumbers. This dip works with whatever smoked fish you have on hand—fatty salmon, delicate trout—and is dairy-free, thanks to Kewpie Mayonnaise. The dip can be eaten immediately but the flavors meld over time, so it's even better when made a few hours or even a couple of days ahead of time.

MAKES 1 CUP

- 8 ounces (225 g) smoked fish, like salmon or trout, chopped
- 3 tablespoons (45 g) finely chopped shallot
- ¼ cup (25 g) finely chopped celery hearts
- 2 tablespoons finely chopped fresh parsley
- 2 tablespoons lemon juice
- 1 teaspoon lemon zest
- 5 tablespoons (75 ml) Kewpie Mayonnaise
- ¼ teaspoon freshly ground black pepper
- Kosher salt, as needed
- Potato chips, cucumber spears, and lemon wedges, for serving

1. In a medium bowl, combine the smoked fish, shallot, celery hearts, parsley, lemon juice, lemon zest, mayonnaise, and black pepper. Mix until fully combined. Season with salt, as needed.

2. Transfer the dip to an airtight container. Let the mixture set in the fridge for a few hours or up to 2 days before serving.

3. Transfer to a serving dish, and eat with potato chips, cucumber spears, and lemon wedges.

The DIP FORMULA

Kewpie Mayonnaise is the perfect base for any dip, and these easy recipes prove it.

A SQUEEZE of KEWPIE MAYONNAISE

- Olive oil + minced garlic → **THE EASIEST AIOLI**
- Chili crisp + fried shallots → **SPICY, CRUNCHY DIP**
- Soy sauce → **HAWAI'I-STYLE SHOYU MAYO**
- Lemon + pinch of salt + freshly ground pepper → **CITRUSY CREAM**

The
PEOPLE BEHIND KEWPIE MAYO

DR. HIDEAKI KOBAYASHI

CURRENT ROLE AT KEWPIE CORPORATION:
Researcher and scientist in the R&D department

What was your first encounter with Kewpie Mayonnaise?
"Since I was a child, Kewpie Mayonnaise was always on my table," Dr. Kobayashi remembers—though he didn't notice it until he went to college and had to cook for himself. One of his first meals was "a salad with lettuce on a plate, a whole can of mackerel on top of it, and a lot of Kewpie Mayonnaise," he explains, adding, "I still remember it not only was nutritious for the body but also the mind."

How did you get started at the company?
"I wanted to make preserved eggs, since there are many disasters in Japan," he says. "So it would be necessary to develop foods that can be stored." Dr. Kobayashi knew Kewpie centered its product on eggs and applied for a job. While he hasn't been able to create his exact dream food product, he has been able to extend the shelf life of Kewpie Mayonnaise, which he considers a "preserved egg food."

What are you working on now?
"Blood sugar–friendly rice," Dr. Kobayashi says. "More than half of the world's population eats rice as their staple food, and this high consumption of white rice is also said to predispose diabetes." So he's been experimenting with adding a small amount of emulsified oil to the rice as it's cooking and monitoring how this affects glucose levels on a test group. "I hope in the future, everyone will be able to eat healthy and delicious onigiri made with this rice," he adds.

How do you cook with Kewpie Mayonnaise at home?
"Kewpie Mayonnaise does not select a partner," Dr. Kobayashi says—meaning, for him, it goes well with everything, from vegetables to fish. "I recommend adding a little Kewpie Mayonnaise when cooking rice," he shares. "This may be a new discovery of the deliciousness of rice."

KEWPIE BY THE DECADE: The 1930s

Making something this good means one thing: competition. A few years after its initial release, demand for Kewpie Mayonnaise skyrocketed, leading to new rivals entering the Japanese market. However, after the Shōwa financial crisis, which was triggered by the Great Depression in America, many competing mayonnaise brands collapsed, while business for Shokuhin Kogyo Co., which would later become Kewpie, boomed. Sales climbed each year during the 1930s, and to keep the creamy condiment flowing, the company expanded its importing, built a second manufacturing plant, and started an egg farm.

Yes, an egg farm. Nakashima and the team realized the company needed a steady supply of high-quality eggs for all the yolk-only mayonnaise being produced and decided to take the matter into their own hands. The team turned a dusty plot of land in Kitatama-gun in Tokyo into Nishifu Farm, complete with wooden coops, local hired hands, and lots of hens wandering around. (Nishifu remains a Kewpie facility today.)

As mayonnaise production increased, a new problem surfaced, one that would continually confound Nakashima for decades: What to do with all the egg whites?! At the

Behind the scenes at Nishifu Farm, Kewpie's egg farm in Tokyo

KEWPIE ON THE RISE

On the production line of Kewpie Mayonnaise, where workers attached labels to bottles

time, Shokuhin Kogyo Co. discarded the egg whites from the used yolks, and as company documents report, this was considered "a grave issue" to Nakashima. As a solution, they began selling leftover egg whites to confection manufacturers and pharmaceutical and printing companies, and later started drying them as separate products. The latter idea ended up being successful enough that a dehydrator was installed at the farm.

However, it turns out that egg whites were a small matter in comparison to the challenges the company faced at the end of the decade. As World War II erupted in Europe, disrupting supply chains worldwide, it became difficult for Shokuhin Kogyo Co. to import the other ingredients, such as oil, that it relied on for making mayonnaise. Soon, Kewpie Mayonnaise started falling short of its production target. The downturn came to a head in 1940, when Japan entered World War II.

Soy-Glazed Chicken Wings

Oven-baked chicken wings are much easier to prepare and less messy to eat than fried or grilled wings, and this recipe avoids the common mishap of overcooking the wings thanks to its moisture-locking marinade. The result of this nearly foolproof method is garlicky, Kewpie-shellacked, sticky-tender wings—no thermometer or anxious checking necessary.

SERVES 4

FOR THE WINGS

- ½ cup (120 ml) Kewpie Mayonnaise
- 2 garlic cloves, minced
- ¼ cup (50 g) raw cane sugar
- 1 teaspoon chili flakes
- 1½ teaspoons kosher salt
- 1 teaspoon freshly ground black pepper
- 2 pounds (900 g) chicken wings, patted dry

FOR THE SAUCE

- 2 tablespoons cornstarch
- ⅓ cup (80 ml) soy sauce
- 1 tablespoon toasted sesame oil
- ¼ cup (60 ml) sake
- ¼ cup (50 g) raw cane sugar
- 2 tablespoons rice vinegar

Toasted sesame seeds, for serving

Sliced green scallions, green parts only, for serving

1. Preheat the oven to 425°F (220°C) and line a baking sheet with parchment paper.
2. In a large bowl, combine the mayonnaise, garlic, raw cane sugar, chili flakes, salt, and black pepper. Add the chicken wings and toss to coat evenly.
3. Place the wings on the baking sheet, spacing them out as much as possible for even browning.
4. Bake the wings for 30 minutes, until golden brown.
5. Make the sauce: In a small bowl, dissolve the cornstarch in 2 tablespoons of water.
6. In a saucepan, combine the soy sauce, sesame oil, sake, raw cane sugar, and rice vinegar. Bring to a boil over medium heat. Whisking constantly, add the cornstarch slurry to the sauce. Let it come back to a boil and cook for an additional minute until thickened.
7. Once the wings are done, transfer to a large bowl and toss them with the sauce until well coated.
8. Garnish with sesame seeds and scallions. Serve immediately.

Potato Takoyaki

Takoyaki is a classic Japanese street food. The octopus-filled fritters hail from Osaka and are piled high with sauces, flakes, and more. The secret ingredient in this cheesy, deep-fried version is mashed potatoes, which are added to the batter, along with potato starch, to prevent the balls from falling apart in the fryer. The takoyaki are finished with the usual suspects: a generous drizzle of Kewpie Mayonnaise and salty-sweet homemade takoyaki sauce, plus a sprinkle of toasty aonori and smoky katsuobushi. Enjoy them as a snack, like you would in Japan, or as an impressive party appetizer.

MAKES 6 TAKOYAKI BALLS

¾ cup (180 ml) Worcestershire sauce

4 teaspoons mentsuyu (concentrated noodle soup base)

3 teaspoons granulated sugar

2 teaspoons ketchup

1 teaspoon cornstarch or potato starch

10½ ounces (300 g) potatoes, peeled and cut into 2-inch (5 cm) cubes

2 teaspoons potato starch

½ teaspoon kosher salt

⅔ cup (80 g) pancake mix

4¼ fluid ounces (120 ml) milk

1 tablespoon Kewpie Mayonnaise, plus more for serving

6 teaspoons (30 g) shredded cheese (mozzarella or Cheddar)

7 ounces (200 g) octopus, cut into ½-inch (12 mm) pieces

Neutral vegetable oil, such as canola, for frying

Aonori (seaweed flakes), for serving

Katsuobushi (bonito flakes), for serving

1. Make the takoyaki sauce: In a small pot, combine the Worcestershire sauce, mentsuyu, sugar, and ketchup. Whisk together. In a small bowl, mix the cornstarch with 1 tablespoon of water, then add it to the pot and whisk. Bring to a boil and cook the takoyaki sauce for 1 minute, then turn off the heat.

2. Bring a pot of water to a boil, and cook the potatoes until soft, about 10 to 15 minutes. Drain and mash while still hot.

3. In a large bowl, combine the mashed potatoes, potato starch, and salt. Mash until smooth and well combined.

4. In a separate bowl, mix the pancake mix with the milk and mayonnaise until smooth.

5. Take 2 tablespoons of the mashed potato mixture and flatten it into a circle. Place 1 teaspoon shredded cheese and 1 piece of octopus in the center. Roll the mixture into a ball, making sure the filling is fully enclosed. Repeat with the remaining potato mixture.

6. Heat a pot over medium-high heat and add enough oil to reach about 3 inches (7 cm) on the side of the pot. Heat the oil to 375°F (190°C). Dip the potato balls into the pancake batter, allowing any excess batter to drip off, and then carefully drop them into the hot oil. Deep-fry until golden brown on all sides, about 4 to 5 minutes.

7. Place the fried balls on a serving plate. Top with the takoyaki sauce, mayonnaise, aonori, and katsuobushi or serve the toppings on the side and garnish to your liking. Enjoy immediately.

Oven-Fried Shrimp

Kewpie is the ultimate secret ingredient to creating a perfect battered-and-fried crunch without a deep fryer. In this recipe for mayo-and-panko-coated shrimp, Kewpie does two things: First, it replaces the usual egg dip, since it has so much yolk. Second, as the mayonnaise heats up in the oven, so does the oil in it, which ends up frying the shrimp and giving the panko crust an irresistible crunch. The result is a snack that's too easy to pop one after another.

MAKES 31 TO 40 SHRIMP

- 1 cup (240 ml) Kewpie Mayonnaise, plus more for serving
- 1 teaspoon garlic powder
- ½ teaspoon white pepper
- ½ teaspoon kosher salt
- 1 cup (100 g) panko bread crumbs
- 1 pound (450 g), about 31 to 40, tail-on shrimp, patted dry
- Japanese barbecue sauce, for serving
- Lemon wedges, for serving

1. Preheat the oven to 425°F (220°C) and line a baking sheet with parchment paper.
2. In a medium bowl, mix the mayonnaise, garlic powder, white pepper, and salt until well combined. Place the panko in a separate shallow dish for dredging.
3. Dip each shrimp into the mayonnaise mixture to coat evenly, then roll in the panko to cover completely. Place the coated shrimp on the prepared baking sheet.
4. Bake for 10 minutes, until the panko is lightly browned.
5. Carefully transfer the warm shrimp to a serving plate using a fish spatula.
6. Serve immediately with Japanese barbecue sauce and mayonnaise for dipping, along with lemon wedges.

Seaweed Fries

These fries are modeled after McDonald's Shake Shake Fries, a popular side at locations throughout Asia. Here's how it works: Get a bag of fries, dump in a flavoring packet, shake the bag vigorously, and enjoy perfectly seasoned fries. Deep-frying fresh potatoes at home can be a daunting task, so instead this recipe starts with frozen fries that are then tossed in furikake, finely chopped garlic, and crushed toasted seaweed. Finish with a zigzag of Kewpie Mayonnaise for a creamy touch and you've got a seriously satisfying side. Pro tip: Crinkle-cut or waffle-cut fries work best here because more surface area equals more seasoning.

SERVES 4

Neutral vegetable oil, such as canola, for frying (optional)

1 32-ounce (900 g) bag frozen crinkle-cut or waffle-cut fries

Two 0.17-ounce (5 g) packages seasoned roasted seaweed, crushed into 1-inch (2 cm) pieces

3 tablespoons (21 g) furikake, plus more for serving

3 garlic cloves, finely chopped

1 tablespoon granulated sugar

½ teaspoon kosher salt

Kewpie Mayonnaise, for serving

Shichimi togarashi or cayenne pepper, for serving

1. Fry or bake the fries according to package directions, until golden brown and crisp.

2. Transfer the hot fries to a large bowl. Immediately sprinkle the crushed seaweed, furikake, garlic, sugar, and salt over the fries. Toss well to coat evenly.

3. Pile the fries in a shallow bowl, topping with any leftover seasoning from the bowl. Drizzle with mayonnaise and sprinkle additional furikake and shichimi togarashi. Serve while still hot.

Buffalo Cauliflower Bites

This is a vegetarian take on classic Buffalo wings, with cauliflower subbing in for the chicken. The cruciferous vegetable gets a crackled, caramelized texture in the oven thanks to two coatings: first, a dip in a garlic-and-cayenne batter, and then a lather in our Buffalo sauce. You'll be tempted to double-dip the Buffalo cauliflower chunks in the blue cheese sauce, which is a richer, more rounded version made with Kewpie Mayonnaise—and we won't tell if you do.

SERVES 4

FOR THE CAULIFLOWER

- 2/3 cup (80 g) all-purpose flour
- 1/4 cup (34 g) cornstarch
- 2 teaspoons garlic powder
- 1/2 teaspoon cayenne pepper
- 1/2 teaspoon kosher salt
- 1 small head cauliflower (about 1 pound/450 g), broken into large florets

FOR THE BUFFALO SAUCE

- 1/2 cup (120 ml) cayenne pepper hot sauce, such as Frank's RedHot
- 4 tablespoons (60 g) unsalted butter, melted
- 2 tablespoons honey
- 1/2 teaspoon white pepper
- 1 teaspoon paprika
- Kosher salt, as needed
- Freshly ground black pepper, as needed

FOR THE BLUE CHEESE SAUCE

- 1 cup (135 g) crumbled blue cheese
- 1/4 cup (60 ml) Kewpie Mayonnaise
- 1/4 cup (60 ml) Greek yogurt or sour cream

1. Preheat the oven to 450°F (230°C) and line two large baking sheets with parchment paper.

2. In a large bowl, whisk together the flour, cornstarch, garlic powder, cayenne pepper, and salt. Add 3/4 cup (180 ml) of water and whisk until smooth. Add the cauliflower florets and stir to coat evenly.

3. Lift the cauliflower florets out of the batter, allowing any excess to drip back into the bowl. Arrange the florets in a single layer on the prepared baking sheets; avoid moving them once placed. Bake for 10 minutes. After 10 minutes, use a fish spatula to carefully flip the florets, and then swap the pans on the oven racks. Bake for another 10 minutes.

4. Make the buffalo sauce: In a medium bowl, stir together the hot sauce, butter, honey, white pepper, and paprika. Season with salt and/or black pepper as needed.

5. Make the blue cheese sauce: In a small bowl, combine the blue cheese, mayonnaise, and Greek yogurt. Stir until smooth.

6. Remove the cauliflower from the oven and brush with some of the Buffalo sauce. Return to the oven and bake for another 12 to 15 minutes, or until the cauliflower is dark and crispy around the edges.

7. Remove the cauliflower from the oven, brush with additional Buffalo sauce, and serve immediately with the blue cheese sauce. Both sauces can be kept in airtight containers in the refrigerator for up to 5 days.

KEWPIE IN THE WORLD

KEWPIE BACKGROUND MUSIC

What does a radio show from a mayonnaise company sound like? Look no further than *Kewpie Background Music*, the Sunday morning radio show that aired in Japan beginning in 1961. It played a mix of easy listening with minimal talk—some of the tracks were even selected by Yuichi Nakashima, the son of founder Toichiro Nakashima and the former Kewpie chairman. For many listeners, it became their actual background music, the kind of chill tunes made for long, lazy weekend breakfasts. And when *Kewpie Background Music* ended in 1990, many called in to share their disappointment. However, Kewpie didn't completely leave the airwaves: Today, a program called the *Kewpie Melody Holiday* airs on Japanese national radio and online during the six national holidays.

These Kewpie Background Music ads from the 1970s teased songs played on air, like Mozart's Serenade.

Listen at
https://www.joqr.co.jp/meloholi/

サラダ おかず

sides salads

SHICHIMI GRILLED CORN 49

GARLIC ROASTED POTATOES 53

CREAMY MASHED POTATOES 55

TOMATO SANDWICH *with* GARLIC MAYONNAISE . . . 59

CAESAR SALAD 62

SESAME WEDGE SALAD 64

COLESLAW 67

AVOCADO TUNA SALAD 68

JAPANESE POTATO SALAD 70

GREEN GODDESS POTATO SALAD 72

Shichimi Grilled Corn

This riff on elote, the Mexican-style grilled corn slathered with mayonnaise and salty cotija, highlights Asian flavors. In this recipe, Kewpie Mayonnaise is mixed with a few pantry staples—oyster sauce, honey, shichimi togarashi—for a salty, sweet, spicy glaze that's more than the sum of its parts. The amped-up mayonnaise is then brushed on the corn before grilling, which lends the cobs an extra-toasty flavor and a golden-brown sheen. (This is due to the proteins in the mayonnaise that brown when heated.) The glaze also works great as a coating for stir-fried tofu or grilled cheese.

SERVES 4

½ cup (120 ml) Kewpie Mayonnaise

1 teaspoon soy sauce

1 tablespoon oyster sauce

1 tablespoon honey

2 teaspoons shichimi togarashi

4 ears corn, husk removed but still attached

1 teaspoon lime zest

4 lime wedges, for serving

1. In a small bowl, mix together the mayonnaise, soy sauce, oyster sauce, honey, and 1 teaspoon shichimi togarashi.

2. Grill the corn over medium-high heat for 12 to 15 minutes, turning and moving around every 2 minutes, until kernels are charred.

3. Brush the mayonnaise mixture evenly onto the corn. Continue to grill for 1 to 2 minutes, turning constantly, until the sauce layer is charred all around.

4. Place the grilled corn on platters, sprinkle with the lime zest and the remaining shichimi togarashi, and serve with the lime wedges.

KEWPIE BY THE DECADE — The 1940s

As World War II unfolded in the Pacific, Kewpie (then called Shokuhin Kogyo Co.) was thrust into the military effort like many Japanese companies at the time. Even if the company wanted to produce mayonnaise on the side, it was impossible, as many employees had entered the draft and essential ingredients were scarce. Plants stopped mixing and bottling mayonnaise and began manufacturing military supplies. Kewpie even developed something called Yolkmin, a yolk-based "nutritious drink" for soldiers.

During the war, a black market materialized to fill in the gaps where rations and inconsistent supply chains failed. For many, the black market was an inextricable part of daily life in Japan, and when the war ended in 1945, it remained a resource as the country recovered. Employees (and likely customers) expected Kewpie Mayonnaise to make its triumphant return immediately, which would have required the company to source ingredients from the black market. However, Nakashima refused. For him, it was a violation of his principles; he didn't want to compromise his product with ingredients that were illegal and of lesser quality. In response, waves of employees quit—a small group even established a competing mayonnaise company.

When Kewpie Mayonnaise started up again in 1948, Nakashima and his son Yuichi were some of the last employees standing. After the five-year hiatus, mayonnaise production was low at first—small enough for

One of Kewpie's high tech (and industry-standard-setting) equipment: an automatic bottle washer

WAR HITS JAPAN—AND KEWPIE

employees to deliver orders by three-wheel van—and as it ramped up, the company had to outsource some of the mayo manufacturing to Aohata Canning, which produced Nakashima's beloved orange marmalade.

Still, Kewpie struggled to get back on its feet financially. Nakashima had to sell personal belongings, and he borrowed aggressively from banks to keep the business afloat. Things were grim until, one day, Nakashima came home to a surprise: a wad of cash, 30,000 yen, wrapped in newspaper. Thanks to this unexpected gift from a friend, Nakashima finally had a glimmer of hope for his company.

Kewpie employees boxing up 50-gram polyethylene bags of mayonnaise

Garlic Roasted Potatoes

Yukon Gold potatoes are made for roasting. Because they have a lot of sugar and not a ton of starch, they easily crisp in the oven while maintaining a fluffy, flavorful flesh. The only thing that makes roasted Yukon Golds even better is a generous dose of Kewpie Mayonnaise and garlic. When the potatoes are tossed in this mixture and then roasted, the mayonnaise deepens the browning and evenly distributes the grated garlic all over the potatoes. This seasoning is versatile; use it as the base for roasting root vegetables such as carrots, sweet potatoes, and parsnips.

SERVES 4

3 tablespoons (45 g) grated garlic

¼ cup (60 ml) Kewpie Mayonnaise

½ teaspoon kosher salt

½ teaspoon freshly ground black pepper

1 pound (450 g) Yukon Gold potatoes, cut into 1- to 2-inch (2 to 4 cm) pieces

1 small block of Parmesan or Pecorino, for serving

1 teaspoon thinly sliced fresh chives, for serving

1. Preheat the oven to 375°F (190°C).
2. In a medium bowl, mix the garlic, mayonnaise, salt, and black pepper. Stir to combine, then add the potatoes and mix until the pieces are evenly coated.
3. Evenly distribute the potatoes onto a baking sheet. Bake in the oven for 20 minutes, flip the potato pieces with a fish spatula, and then return them to the oven for another 15 to 20 minutes, until the potatoes are golden brown and cooked through.
4. Transfer the potatoes to a platter or shallow bowl. Grate the cheese onto the hot potatoes, then garnish with the chives. Serve immediately.

Creamy Mashed Potatoes

Mashing potatoes can be a tedious and laborious task, but it's no match for the powers of Kewpie mayo. The egg yolks and oil in the condiment kick-start the creaming process, so you can easily incorporate the cooked potatoes with the mayonnaise, which immediately gives them a velvety consistency, as well as a rich, slightly tangy flavor. This recipe finishes the mashed potatoes with a crack of white pepper and chopped chives, but feel free to use whatever seasonings and toppings you prefer.

SERVES 6 TO 8

- 4 pounds (1.8 kg) Yukon Gold potatoes, peeled and cut into 1-inch (2 cm) pieces
- 2 tablespoons kosher salt
- ½ cup (115 g) unsalted butter
- 1 cup (240 ml) whole milk
- ½ cup (120 ml) Kewpie Mayonnaise
- 3 tablespoons (9 g) chopped fresh chives
- ½ teaspoon white pepper

1. Place the potatoes in a large pot and pour in enough water to cover. Add a generous pinch of salt and set the pot over high heat. Bring to a boil, then reduce the heat to medium and simmer until the potatoes are fork-tender, about 15 to 20 minutes. Drain the potatoes.

2. In the same pot, melt the butter in the milk over medium-low heat. Remove from the heat. Smash the potatoes with a potato masher or press them through a ricer and into the pot, mixing well. Fold in the mayonnaise, add half of the chives, and season with the salt and white pepper. Transfer the mashed potatoes to a serving dish, sprinkle the rest of the chives on top, and eat while still warm.

Kewpie by the Decade: The 1950s

Polyethylene bags came in boxes (top) to protect the mayo from dust and direct sunlight.

The newly designed plastic Kewpie bottles in play

After the war, Kewpie Mayonnaise was back up and running, and Nakashima was more focused than ever. He personally inspected imported oils to make sure they met his standard for production, and he maintained extremely high levels of cleanliness at the factories and installed state-of-the-art equipment. Every evening, after a long day of work at the factories, he met with employees to listen to any issues that came up and to share his vision of making a mayonnaise that would strengthen and nourish Japanese people. His effort paid off. By 1952, Kewpie Mayonnaise had surpassed its prewar peak in production and sales.

Around this time, the Kewpie brand we now know (and love) started to crystallize. In 1957, Shokuhin Kogyo Co. officially changed its name to Kewpie Corporation. "Shokuhin kogyo" means "food industry," and Nakashima imagined this name would be confusing with more food companies popping up in Japan. As he was thinking of a new name, he had three stipulations: It needed to be a word that worked in both Japanese and English, didn't have "shokuhin" in it, and must match with the product. So, Kewpie it was.

In 1956, Kewpie had tested out polyethylene bags, which were lightweight and easy to handle, and found that they kept out oxygen better than the lidded glass containers the company had been using. Customers seemed to love the packaging, too, buying up more mayo than expected. Kewpie debuted its now-iconic plastic bottle in 1958. The first teardrop-shaped container was nearly identical to today's packaging: a soft, squeezable bottle with a red cap.

KEWPIE REBUILDS

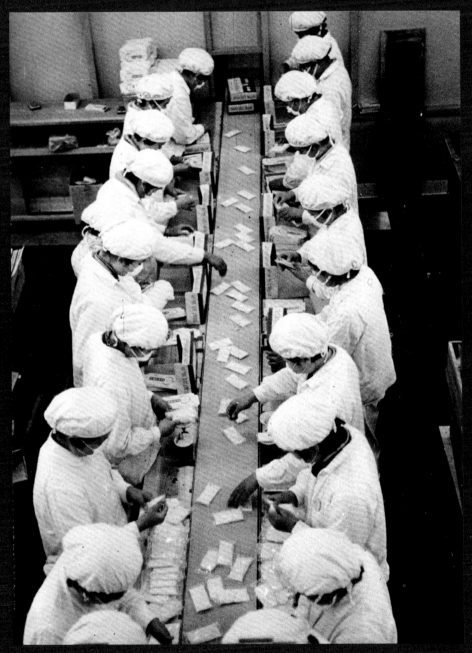

Kewpie employees boxing up polyethylene bags of mayonnaise, a precursor to today's plastic bottles

Tomato Sandwich *with* Garlic Mayonnaise

The best way to enjoy tomatoes at their peak is simply, and that's why the tomato-and-mayo sandwich is such a cult favorite in the American South and beyond. This version plays up the umami of the sandwich, but don't worry—it's just as easy to whip up as the original. Stirring fresh grated garlic into the mayo adds a punchy savoriness that goes well with the thick, juicy tomato slices and white bread. This is a no-cook snack you'll make on repeat all summer long.

SERVES 1

- Two ½-inch-thick (12 mm) slices beefsteak tomato
- ¼ teaspoon kosher salt
- ¼ teaspoon freshly ground black pepper
- 3 tablespoons (45 ml) Kewpie Mayonnaise
- 1 tablespoon grated garlic
- 2 slices white sandwich bread

1. Arrange tomato slices in a single layer, and sprinkle evenly with the salt and black pepper. Let stand for 3 to 5 minutes. Using paper towels, lightly pat dry both sides of tomato slices, and set aside.
2. Mix the mayonnaise with the garlic.
3. Spread one side of each bread slice with the mayonnaise mixture.
4. Arrange tomato slices on the mayo side of one bread slice; top with the other bread slice, mayo side down. Enjoy immediately.

KEWPIE PATTERNS

Your plate is a canvas, whether it's holding day-old fried rice, a quick sandwich, or pasta that could use some pizzazz—and Kewpie is your paintbrush. Each bottle of Kewpie Mayonnaise comes with two tips built in that give you the precision (and the flourish) to make whatever you're eating a little more fun.

THIN TIP — This is in the red cap!

STAR TIP — Unscrew the cap for this thicker, ridged tip built into the bottle itself.

- Stripes
- Crosshatch
- Swirls
- Squiggles

- Puffs
- Outline
- Thick lines
- Dots

THAILAND

EUROPE

NORTH AMERICA

MALAYSIA

CHINA

INDONESIA

VIETNAM

KEWPIE BOTTLE DESIGNS ACROSS *the* GLOBE

The design of the Kewpie bottle varies slightly in different countries depending on available materials and local design preferences for the country in which it's produced. Above is a little preview of the different Kewpie bottles out in the world.

SIDES AND SALADS ◆ 61

Caesar Salad

Homemade Caesar dressing typically relies on a finicky process of slowly mixing oil into a raw egg yolk. Rather than going through the trouble of emulsifying (i.e., vigorously stirring these two ingredients) by hand, this recipe uses mayonnaise as a shortcut. Kewpie provides the essential creamy, tangy base, without the worry of breaking the emulsification. And because there are no raw eggs, this dressing keeps much longer than a typical fresh Caesar.

SERVES 4

- 2 tablespoons unsalted butter
- ½ cup (60 g) panko bread crumbs
- ½ teaspoon kosher salt, plus more as needed
- Freshly ground black pepper, as needed
- 1 tablespoon finely grated lemon zest
- 2 oil-packed anchovy fillets
- ¼ cup (60 ml) lemon juice
- 3 tablespoons (45 ml) Kewpie Mayonnaise
- 1 teaspoon Dijon mustard
- 1 teaspoon Worcestershire sauce
- 2 garlic cloves, finely grated
- ½ cup (50 g) finely grated Parmesan, plus more for serving
- ¼ cup (60 ml) extra-virgin olive oil
- 2 medium romaine lettuce hearts (about 8 ounces/227 g)

1. Make the bread crumb topping: In a medium skillet over medium heat, melt the butter. Add the panko, ¼ teaspoon salt, and a few grinds of black pepper. Cook the panko, stirring often but being careful not to crush, until golden brown, 5 to 8 minutes. Carefully stir in half of the lemon zest and set aside.

2. Using the flat side of a chef's knife, smash the anchovy fillets to a coarse paste; transfer paste to a medium bowl. Whisk in the lemon juice, mayonnaise, Dijon mustard, Worcestershire sauce, garlic, Parmesan, and remaining salt. Gradually stream in the olive oil, whisking constantly until dressing is smooth and creamy.

3. Halve romaine lettuce hearts lengthwise, then cut crosswise into 1-inch (2 cm) strips and place into a large bowl. Add half of the dressing to the bowl with lettuce and toss to coat evenly. Taste and add more dressing by the tablespoonful until the salad is well dressed. Taste salad and season with more salt and black pepper if needed.

4. Mound salad onto a platter or divide among plates. Drizzle any remaining dressing over salad and top with more Parmesan, bread crumb topping, and remaining lemon zest.

Sesame Wedge Salad

This is a minimalist's wedge salad with a Japanese twist. It has all the wonderful things about the classic dish—big chunks of iceberg lettuce that require a fork and knife, an intense and rich salad dressing, and textural bits—but without the unwieldy loaded-baked-potato level of toppings. Just stir together sesame paste with Japanese pantry essentials (Kewpie Mayonnaise, rice vinegar, soy sauce) and chop up a head of lettuce—that's it! Finish this sesame-forward, streamlined wedge with furikake, or in a pinch, toasted sesame seeds and crushed roasted seaweed.

SERVES 6

¼ cup (60 ml) sesame paste or tahini

¾ cup (180 ml) Kewpie Mayonnaise

½ cup (120 ml) rice vinegar

2 tablespoons soy sauce

4 teaspoons granulated sugar

1 teaspoon mirin

1 tablespoon toasted sesame oil

1 large head iceberg lettuce (about 2¼ pounds/1 kg), outer leaves removed, cut into 6 wedges

¼ cup (28 g) furikake

1. Combine the sesame paste, mayonnaise, rice vinegar, soy sauce, sugar, mirin, and sesame oil in a medium bowl and whisk together.

2. Arrange lettuce wedges on plates. Pour about ¼ cup (60 ml) dressing over each wedge. Sprinkle each with the furikake. Serve the remaining dressing on the side.

GETTING EVERY LAST DROP

Still have some Kewpie Mayonnaise left in the bottle? This is a common conundrum among Kewpie Mayonnaise lovers: You've squeezed and squeezed and squeezed, and now your bottle is almost empty. But there's still a *tiny* bit left, so how do you get to those last gloops of mayonnaise?

The solution isn't to keep squeezing, but to actually add stuff to the bottle. Throw some oil and vinegar into the bottle along with ingredients such as minced herbs, grated garlic, a dose of soy sauce—whatever speaks to you. Shake everything up, and boom: You've got a creamy dressing that's perfect for jazzing up a simple salad or finishing a bowl of instant noodles.

Coleslaw

Let's face it, too many coleslaws are soggy and bland. But not this perky slaw, which stays nice and crisp after salting the cabbage, shallot, and carrot ahead of time to draw out any excess water. The dressing is an intensely savory (in a good way) flavor bomb of Kewpie Mayonnaise, two kinds of vinegar, a little sugar, and grated ginger. The latter adds a subtle spicy pop that balances out this creamy, crunchy salad. It'll soon become an essential for any picnic or barbecue.

SERVES 6

- ½ large head green cabbage (about 2 pounds/900 g), cored and finely shredded
- 2 large shallots (about 4 ounces/115 g), thinly sliced
- 1 large carrot (about 6 ounces/170 g), peeled and coarsely grated
- ¼ cup thinly sliced scallions (about 1 ounce/30 g), plus more for serving
- ½ cup plus 1 tablespoon granulated sugar (about 130 g), plus more as needed
- ¼ cup kosher salt (about 60 g), plus more as needed
- ½ cup Kewpie Mayonnaise (120 ml)
- 2 teaspoons grated ginger
- 1 tablespoon rice vinegar, plus more as needed
- 1 tablespoon white vinegar, plus more as needed
- 1 tablespoon Dijon mustard
- 1 teaspoon white pepper, plus more as needed

1. Combine the cabbage, shallots, carrot, and scallions (reserve some scallion greens for serving) in a large bowl, leaving enough room to toss. Sprinkle with ½ cup sugar and salt, and toss to combine. Let the mixture rest for 5 minutes.

2. After resting, transfer the mixture to a large colander and rinse thoroughly under cold water to remove excess salt and sugar.

3. Transfer the rinsed vegetables to a salad spinner and spin dry. Alternatively, spread them on a large rimmed baking sheet lined with paper towels or a clean kitchen towel, and blot them dry with more paper towels. Return the dried vegetables to the large bowl and set aside.

4. In a medium bowl, combine the mayonnaise, ginger, rice vinegar, white vinegar, Dijon mustard, white pepper, and the remaining sugar. Whisk until smooth and homogeneous.

5. Pour the dressing over the cabbage mixture and toss to coat evenly. Taste and adjust seasoning with more salt, white pepper, sugar, and/or vinegar if desired. Garnish with the reserved scallion greens before serving, or store in an airtight container in the refrigerator for up to 5 days.

Avocado Tuna Salad

Can tuna salad be elegant? This avocado-and-allium-laden version answers that question with an emphatic yes. The tuna salad is tossed with avocado chunks (some mashed and seasoned, guacamole-style) and a fragrant mix of shallots, cilantro, and lemon zest. The most important ingredient, though, is the tuna: Make sure to use tinned fish that is stored in oil, for a richer flavor and luscious texture. The second most important ingredient is Kewpie Mayonnaise, which not only binds the shredded tuna together but also gives it a light but fatty flavor to go with the rest of the ingredients. Now this is one sophisticated tuna salad (shown on page 68).

SERVES 4 TO 6

Two 6-ounce (170 g) cans oil-packed tuna, drained

2 tablespoons Kewpie Mayonnaise

2 teaspoons lemon juice, plus more as needed

1 shallot (about 5 ounces/140 g), sliced into thin half-circles

2 stalks celery, chopped

¼ cup (15 g) chopped fresh cilantro

1 medium lemon, zested

1 medium avocado

1 teaspoon grated garlic

2 tablespoons chopped fresh chives

3 tablespoons (45 ml) extra-virgin olive oil, plus more as needed

½ teaspoon kosher salt, plus more as needed

¼ teaspoon freshly ground black pepper

1. Drain the tuna and place it in a large bowl with the mayonnaise and half of the lemon juice. Break up any large chunks of tuna with a fork, mixing it with the mayonnaise.

2. Add the shallot, celery, cilantro, and lemon zest to the bowl.

3. Halve and pit the avocado. Cut one half into ⅓- to ¼-inch (1 cm) pieces and add to the bowl with the tuna. Gently mix until well combined, trying to keep the avocado pieces intact.

4. In a medium bowl, put the other avocado half, remaining lemon juice, and garlic. Use a whisk to mash the avocado, then stir until smooth.

5. Add the chives, olive oil, salt, and black pepper to the smooth avocado mixture. Whisk until smooth and well combined.

6. Transfer the avocado mixture to the bowl with the tuna and gently mix until everything is evenly coated. Taste and adjust the seasoning with more lemon juice, olive oil, and salt as needed. Serve as is or on your bread of choice, and enjoy as soon as possible or within 1 day.

KEWPIE IN THE WORLD

MOTHERS' CHORUS FESTIVAL

Since 1978, Kewpie has sponsored the Japan Choral Association's Mothers' Chorus Festival. What's the connection between mayonnaise and singing, you ask? It's simply because Kewpie wanted busy moms (arguably one of its primary customer groups) to "enjoy singing in a chorus to their heart's content." The company is the main sponsor of the annual festival, which showcases thousands of singing troupes made up of Japanese mothers. These kinds of choral societies are popular in Japan, with female groups in particular growing. Kewpie goes beyond just financial support though; in the past, several choral groups would visit the office before the festival to learn how to make mayonnaise. Nothing soothes the vocal cords quite like mayonnaise.

A choir of mothers singing their hearts out, complete with matching outfits, from 2015

Japanese Potato Salad

Creamy, mild, and crunchy, Japanese potato salad is distinct from its mustardy German and pickle-laden American counterparts. Every family in Japan has their own recipe, but it's typically loaded with colorful, fresh vegetables, sometimes ham and a boiled egg. What's always present is Kewpie Mayonnaise, which gives the dish a distinctive tang and savory roundedness. This version incorporates crisp cucumbers and corn, tender ham, and chunky potatoes for a textural delight. You can scoop it onto bread for a sandwich or add it to a light brunch spread—just make sure you enjoy it right away.

SERVES 4

1 medium English cucumber (about 6 ounces/170 g) or 2 whole mini cucumbers, thinly sliced, plus more as needed

1 teaspoon kosher salt, plus more as needed

3 large potatoes (about 1½ pounds/680 g), cut into 1-inch (2 cm) chunks (about 3 cups)

⅓ cup diced ¼-inch (6 mm) carrots (about 3 ounces/85 g)

⅓ cup (about 80 ml) Kewpie Mayonnaise

1½ teaspoons rice vinegar

¼ teaspoon freshly ground black pepper

1 teaspoon granulated sugar

2 hard-boiled eggs, chopped

⅓ cup (about 3 ounces/85 g) sweet corn kernels, canned or fresh

3 slices ham or cooked bacon, diced

½ teaspoon thinly sliced fresh chives

1. Sprinkle the cucumber slices with ½ teaspoon salt to draw out moisture, about 10 minutes. Squeeze out the liquid and set aside.

2. Bring a pot of water to a boil with a large pinch of salt. Add the potatoes and cook until easily pierced with a fork, about 10 to 12 minutes. Add the carrots during the last 2 minutes of cooking to soften them up. Drain and set aside.

3. In a large bowl, combine the mayonnaise, rice vinegar, black pepper, sugar, and remaining salt. Taste and adjust the seasoning of the dressing as needed.

4. Add the cucumber, potatoes, carrots, eggs, corn, and ham to the bowl with the dressing. Stir gently with a large spoon, mashing the potatoes to your desired texture.

5. Transfer to a serving bowl, garnish with the chives, and add more cucumber slices if desired. Serve immediately as is or make into a sandwich with bread.

Green Goddess Potato Salad

Potato salad, meet Green Goddess. The classic side gets a jolt of verdant flavor (and color) from this herb-packed salad dressing. Whir together all the green things—scallion, dill, parsley—with lemon, garlic, and a good amount of Kewpie Mayonnaise. Oftentimes Green Goddess dressing has capers or anchovies, but here Kewpie provides that vinegary punch and savory depth. You can prepare all the elements of this recipe beforehand: Store the dressed potatoes separately from the fresh herbs and halved eggs and assemble everything once you're ready to serve.

SERVES 4

1½ pounds (680 g) baby potatoes, scrubbed

2 teaspoons kosher salt, plus more as needed

¾ cup (60 g) thinly sliced scallions

½ cup (about 15 g) chopped fresh dill sprigs

1 cup (30 g) chopped fresh parsley leaves with tender stems

4 garlic cloves

Zest and juice of 1 medium lemon

½ cup (120 ml) Kewpie Mayonnaise

½ cup (120 ml) sour cream

¼ cup (60 ml) extra-virgin olive oil, plus more as needed

1½ teaspoons freshly ground black pepper, plus more as needed

2 large eggs, soft-boiled and halved

1. Place the baby potatoes in a large pot and cover with water. Add a generous pinch of salt. Bring the water to a boil over high heat, then reduce to medium heat and simmer until the potatoes are fork-tender, about 15 to 20 minutes. Drain the potatoes.

2. In a small bowl, combine ¼ cup (30 g) scallions, ¼ cup dill (8 g), and ¼ cup (7 g) parsley. Toss to mix and set aside.

3. In a blender, combine the remaining scallions, dill, and parsley with 1 teaspoon kosher salt, garlic, lemon zest and juice, mayonnaise, sour cream, olive oil, and black pepper. Blend on high speed for about 2 minutes until smooth.

4. If the potatoes are larger than bite-size, cut them in half. In a large bowl, combine the potatoes with the dressing and toss until evenly coated. Reserve ¼ cup of the herb mixture for serving, add the remaining herb mixture to the potato salad, and toss to combine. Season with more salt, as needed. Cover and chill the salad for at least 2 hours (and up to 1 day) in the refrigerator.

5. When ready to serve, top the potato salad with the halved eggs and the reserved herb mixture. Season with more black pepper, and drizzle with extra olive oil if desired.

Kewpie by the Decade: The 1960s

The egg, inside and out, was the muse of this 1968 ad campaign highlighting Kewpie's prime supply.

During this time, Kewpie solidified itself not only as a cult condiment in Japan but a cultural icon. In 1961, the company started its own radio show called *Kewpie Background Music* (see page 45) and began offering tours of its mayonnaise factories, at the request of elementary students. (Now there is Mayoterrace, a dedicated Kewpie museum; see page 155.) The company invested more in advertising that highlighted the quality of the eggs in Kewpie's mayonnaise, and launched *Three-Minute Cooking* (page 95), a daily TV segment that shows how to cook a nutritious dish from scratch in just a few minutes. Yuichi Nakashima, the founder's son, came up with the idea, and today it's one of the longest-running cooking shows in Japan.

    Behind the scenes, Nakashima Sr. dialed in every aspect of Kewpie Mayonnaise. When production began, Nakashima couldn't find any Western-style vinegars in Japan, so he had collaborated with domestic breweries to make vinegar out of sake lees and rice for his mayo. In 1962, Nakashima established his own company, Nishifu Industries Co., to finally make the Western-style vinegar he dreamed of—using apple juice and malt—exclusively for Kewpie Mayonnaise. In the same regard, Nakashima created separate companies to support almost all aspects of Kewpie production and distribution: Shokuhin Yuso Co. for transporting and storing oil, Kewpie Souko Corporation for storing ingredients, and Kewpie Warehouse

KEWPIE SPREADS ITS WINGS

Transport Co. for holding the finished product, to name a few.

As Kewpie Corporation moved operations in-house, a formidable competitor emerged. Ajinomoto, the Japanese food titan famous for its MSG (monosodium glutamate), entered the mayo market in 1968. Sensing the rivalry unnerved staff, an eighty-four-year-old Nakashima assured employees: "Though old in body, I will pit myself against our giant rival, and work together with you to deal with difficulties without flinching." Some might say a mayo-off had been declared.

A snapshot of just how many oil drums needed to be stored and at the ready for making Kewpie Mayonnaise and more

麺 ご飯

rice noodles

SESAME SALMON ONIGIRI 79

TORCHED SALMON DON 80

SPICY TUNA RICE BOWL 85

CALIFORNIA ROLL 86

SUSHI BAKE. 89

EGG FRIED RICE 90

FISH ROE UDON 92

INSTANTLY CREAMY RAMEN 98

YAKISOBA 101

CARBONARA 102

SPAGHETTI AND MEATBALLS. 109

BAKED MAC AND CHEESE 110

Sesame Salmon Onigiri

These triangular rice balls are the ultimate portable snack. This version doubles down on flavor, mixing the mayonnaise with flaked salmon and sesame paste. If you're not eating them right away, keep the rice balls covered in the fridge and wrap the nori around them once you're ready.

MAKES 4 ONIGIRI

1 tablespoon sesame paste or tahini

2 tablespoons Kewpie Mayonnaise

1 cooked salmon fillet (about 150 g)

1 teaspoon kosher salt, plus more as needed

4 cups (680 g) cooked Japanese short-grain white rice, warm

1 sheet nori (dried laver seaweed), cut into 4 (2-by-5-inch/ 5-by-12 cm) strips

Shichimi togarashi, for serving

1. In a medium bowl, whisk together the sesame paste and mayonnaise. Flake the cooked salmon fillet with a fork and mix it into the sauce. Season with the salt, plus more as needed.

2. Prepare a small bowl of water for wetting your hands. Wet both palms with water, then sprinkle some salt on your hands.

3. Scoop about ½ cup (120 g) warm rice into your nondominant hand. Create a small well in the center of the rice. Add 2 tablespoons of the salmon mixture into the well.

4. Scoop another ½ cup (120 g) rice and cover the filling completely. Mold the rice with your hands to form a ball, gently pressing the rice around the filling.

5. With your dominant hand, form a V shape and place it on top of the rice ball. Gently press to form a triangle corner. Continue pressing and rotating the onigiri, creating the other triangle corners by gently rotating and pressing the sides. Press and rotate the onigiri 2 to 3 more times to finish shaping it.

6. Turn the rice ball on its side and press gently to flatten the sides. Transfer the shaped onigiri to a baking sheet or plate lined with parchment paper. Repeat with the remaining rice and filling.

7. Just before serving, wrap each onigiri with a strip of nori. Sprinkle with shichimi togarashi and eat right away.

Torched Salmon Don

Heating mayonnaise may not seem like the most intuitive use of the ingredient, but the result is a thing of magic. In this recipe, marinated salmon fillets are finished with a mayonnaise-charged sauce and then torched, which intensifies the sweet and savory notes of the condiment while also caramelizing the surface. You need a high, concentrated heat for this effect, which means you'll need to dig out (or buy) a butane-powered kitchen torch. It's worth the investment. Once you try this torched mayonnaise method, you'll want to finish all your proteins this way.

SERVES 2

- 3 tablespoons (45 ml) Kewpie Mayonnaise
- 2 teaspoons sriracha
- 1 teaspoon ketchup
- 1 teaspoon oyster sauce
- 2 tablespoons soy sauce
- 2 tablespoons sake
- 2 salmon fillets (about 8 ounces/225 g total), sliced into ½-inch-thick (12 mm) slices
- 3 cups (511 g) cooked short-grain rice
- 2 tablespoons thinly sliced scallions
- 2 lime wedges, for serving

1. In a small bowl, combine the mayonnaise, sriracha, ketchup, and oyster sauce. Stir well to combine and set the sauce aside.
2. In a medium bowl, mix the soy sauce and sake. Add the salmon and marinate for 5 minutes.
3. Lay the slices of salmon flat on a heatproof tray. Using a kitchen torch, sear the top side of the salmon until it becomes opaque and slight char marks appear. Flip the salmon slices with a small offset spatula or fork and torch the other side.
4. Divide the cooked rice evenly between two heatproof serving bowls. Arrange the cooked salmon slices over the rice, covering it as much as possible.
5. Spoon a thick layer of the sauce over the salmon and any rice peeking through. Torch the salmon until char marks appear on top.
6. Garnish the bowls with the scallions and serve with the lime wedges on the side. Enjoy immediately.

Kewpie by the Decade: The 1970s

At the dawn of what would become a pivotal moment for the company, Kewpie faced a new challenge. The newest competitor, Ajinomoto, captured the mayonnaise market with flashy TV commercials, and Kewpie responded with the Kewpie, naturally. In 1970, the company held a contest—"buy Kewpie Mayonnaise, get a Kewpie doll"—and more than 1.5 million people participated, with 20,000 lucky winners receiving the coveted dolls.

Energized by the boost in sales, Kewpie met customers' enthusiasm by seeking out innovations to make the mayonnaise better than ever. The Kewpie bottle was updated to add an EVOH (ethylene vinyl alcohol) layer, which further prevents oxygen from coming in, and fitted a unique star-shaped tip underneath the cap. The company also lowered prices as it streamlined its operations and manufacturing. Wholesale partners embraced these changes, continuing to promote Kewpie products. In the end, Kewpie Mayonnaise held its ground in the Japanese mayonnaise world. Nakashima later reflected: "Due to the appearance of Ajinomoto Mayonnaise, we had a very hard time competing in the market. Thanks to this, however, Kewpie has made marked progress in many ways."

Throughout the 1970s, Kewpie continued to make moves. Despite Nakashima's initial lack of interest in public funding, Kewpie eventually went public and was listed on the Tokyo Stock Exchange. This enabled the company to raise funds to build more plants and to launch more non-mayo-related products, like a low-sugar version of Nakashima's beloved Aohata orange marmalade.

However, December 19, 1973, marked the end of an era. Nakashima passed away at the age of ninety. He worked as the chairman up until his death and told those close to him not to hold a company funeral. A few days later, his son Yuichi, who became the chairman, did so anyway, as family, friends, colleagues, and employees wanted to pay their respects. Still, Nakashima had the last word: He wrote his own obituary.

This low-sugar orange marmalade, Nakashima's second love, was the first of its kind in Japan.

KEWPIE STANDS ITS GROUND

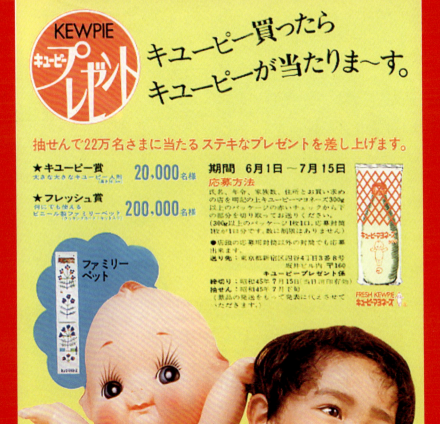

Marketing material (and detailed instructions) for Kewpie fans to enter to win their own Kewpie doll

Spicy Tuna Rice Bowl

This spicy tuna bowl is perfect for picnics or easy lunches at home. The recipe comes together in just two steps but is packed with big-flavor ingredients. Canned tuna is thoroughly and intensely seasoned with a sauce made from pantry staples, then served over warm rice and topped with fresh crunchy cucumbers and sesame seeds. It's a complete meal, simple but satisfying. Rather than reserve the seaweed snacks for topping, you can keep them whole and use them like lettuce wraps to get a perfectly loaded bite.

SERVES 2

One 5-ounce (140 g) can tuna (preferably oil-packed), drained

2 tablespoons Kewpie Mayonnaise

1 tablespoon sriracha

1 tablespoon soy sauce

½ teaspoon rice vinegar

½ teaspoon toasted sesame oil

3 cups (511 g) cooked sushi rice

1 mini cucumber, sliced

1 pack seaweed snack

¼ cup (30 g) thinly sliced scallions

1 teaspoon toasted sesame seeds

2 teaspoons chili crisp

1. In a medium bowl, combine the tuna, mayonnaise, sriracha, soy sauce, rice vinegar, and sesame oil. Mix well and refrigerate until ready to use; it's good for up to 2 days if you're meal-prepping.

2. To assemble the bowls, divide the rice and spicy tuna into 2 serving bowls. Add the cucumber slices and seaweed snack, and garnish with the scallions, sesame seeds, and the chili crisp. Serve immediately.

California Roll

This Canadian invention (and now American icon) isn't always made with mayonnaise. However, not only does the condiment flavor the dish, but it helps bind all the ingredients for easier rolling. To simplify your sushi-forming experience, it's best to use a bamboo sushi mat to better control the tightness of the roll. They're available for purchase at Asian grocery stores and online.

SERVES 4

4 cups (680 g) freshly cooked sushi rice

2 tablespoons seasoned rice vinegar

4 ounces (115 g) cooked or canned crabmeat or imitation crabmeat, shredded

4 teaspoons Kewpie Mayonnaise

2 sheets nori (dried laver seaweed), cut into 4 half sheets

2 tablespoons toasted sesame seeds

1 avocado, cut into ¼-inch (6 mm) slices, rubbed with lemon juice

1 Persian cucumber, seeded and cut into quarters lengthwise

Soy sauce, wasabi, and gari (pickled ginger), for serving

1. As soon as the rice has finished cooking, pour the seasoned rice vinegar all over it: Using a rice paddle or spatula, gently fold the vinegar into the hot rice, separating any chunks. Cover the rice with a lid to keep warm.

2. In a small bowl, combine the crabmeat and mayonnaise. Mix until evenly incorporated.

3. Lay a sheet of plastic wrap over the front and back surfaces of the bamboo sushi mat. Wet a 1-cup (240 ml) measuring cup in a bowl of water, then fill it with sushi rice.

4. Lay a nori half sheet, shiny side down, on the sushi mat. Wet your fingers in the water bowl and evenly spread 1 cup (240 ml) sushi rice across the nori. Sprinkle the rice with ½ tablespoon (9 g) sesame seeds.

5. Flip the nori sheet over so the sushi rice is now facing down on the sushi mat. Align the nori about 1 inch (2 cm) away from the bottom edge of the mat. Place ¼ of the crab mixture, avocado slices, and cucumber strips along the width of the nori, about ½ inch (1 cm) from the bottom edge.

6. Grasp the bottom edge of the bamboo mat with your index fingers and thumbs while holding the filling in place with your other fingers. Roll the sushi mat over the filling until the rice at the bottom edge meets the nori at the top edge. Flip back the mat's bottom edge toward you.

7. Gently squeeze the roll through the mat with one hand while pulling the top of the mat away from you with the other hand. Continue rolling the sushi forward, maintaining gentle pressure with your thumbs and fingers to form a compact roll.

8. Carefully transfer the roll to a tray and cover it to prevent it from drying out. Continue assembling the remaining rolls in the same manner.

9. Using a sharp knife, cut each roll into 8 pieces. Clean the knife after every few cuts. If needed, place the sushi mat over the cut roll, gently reshaping it. Serve immediately with soy sauce and wasabi for dipping, along with gari on the side.

★ **A DISH POWERED BY KEWPIE** ★

Recipes for this viral potluck staple vary, but Kewpie Mayonnaise is nonnegotiable. A sushi bake is decadent to say the least, and Kewpie's light creaminess and vinegary zing cuts through the richness, whereas sour cream and cream cheese can weigh it down further. No matter how one builds a sushi bake, the dish remains a creamy comfort food enjoyed worldwide.

Sushi Bake

What do you get when sushi is transformed into a hearty casserole, baked and bubbling like lasagna? Meet the sushi bake: sushi rice layered with a mixture of cream cheese and crab (or shrimp), then baked, scooped onto seaweed squares, and topped with avocado and Kewpie. The result is something like a warm, creamy, reconstructed California roll that can be eaten with your hands as a main (or rather substantial snack). It's easy to change up the protein in this sushi bake; you can sub in cooked tuna or salmon or even crumbled tofu.

SERVES 4

- ¾ cup (180 ml) Kewpie Mayonnaise
- 2 tablespoons sambal
- 2 tablespoons sriracha
- 1¼ teaspoons toasted sesame oil
- ½ teaspoon granulated sugar
- 2 teaspoons lime juice
- 1 pound (450 g) crabmeat or shrimp, chopped into ¼-inch (6 mm) pieces
- ¼ cup (60 g) cream cheese, room temperature
- 1 tablespoon minced garlic
- 1 tablespoon soy sauce
- 1 teaspoon fish sauce
- 4 cups (720 g) cooked sushi rice
- 7 sheets nori (dried laver seaweed)
- 1 avocado, sliced
- ¼ cup (25 g) thinly sliced scallions
- 1 teaspoon toasted sesame seeds

1. Preheat oven to 425°F (220°C).
2. In a small bowl, mix together ½ cup (120 ml) mayonnaise, sambal, 1 tablespoon sriracha, ¼ teaspoon sesame oil, sugar, and 1 teaspoon lime juice. Stir until smooth and creamy. Set aside.
3. In a medium bowl, combine the crabmeat, cream cheese, garlic, soy sauce, fish sauce, and remaining mayonnaise, sriracha, sesame oil, and lime juice. Mix until everything is evenly incorporated.
4. Line a 9-by-9-inch (23-by-23 cm) baking dish with parchment paper. Spread the cooked sushi rice in an even layer at the bottom of the dish. Tear 1 sheet of nori into bite-sized pieces and sprinkle it over the rice. Then, spread the crabmeat mixture evenly on top.
5. Place the baking dish in the oven and bake for about 10 to 15 minutes, until golden on top. Meanwhile, cut 5 of the nori sheets into 3-inch (7 cm) pieces. Tear the remaining sheet of nori into bite-sized pieces.
6. Once the dish is out of the oven, drizzle with the spicy mayo. Garnish with the avocado, scallions, sesame seeds, and bite-sized nori pieces, and serve with the 3-inch (7 cm) nori sheets for eating as a handheld.

Egg Fried Rice

Fried rice sounds simple, but in reality, the dish requires time, skill, and importantly, a wok. This recipe achieves fried rice perfection without all those things, thanks to Kewpie Mayonnaise. When mixed with rice, the condiment does a few crucial things: It separates the grains so you don't need the usual day-old rice (just cooled rice); it coats each grain for perfectly piece-y (not clumpy) fried rice; and it gives the overall dish the right amount of fat and flavor. Feel free to add diced shrimp, chicken, or tofu along with your favorite vegetables—just be sure to pat dry any wet ingredients before stir-frying with the rice and scallion whites.

SERVES 2

3 tablespoons (45 ml) Kewpie Mayonnaise

2 cups (340 g) cooked short-grain rice, cooled to room temperature

¼ cup (25 g) sliced scallions, whites and greens separated

2 large eggs, beaten

½ teaspoon white pepper

½ teaspoon kosher salt, plus more as needed

1. In a small bowl, mix the mayonnaise with the cooked rice until fully coated.

2. Heat a nonstick pan over medium-high heat, add the rice and scallion whites, and stir-fry for a few minutes until fragrant.

3. Push the rice mixture to one side of the pan. Add the eggs to the other side and scramble until half-cooked. Season with the white pepper and salt, then stir the eggs into the rice mixture.

4. Fold in the scallion greens. Season as needed and serve.

5 WAYS KEWPIE MAYO adds OOMPH

This condiment can do more than drizzle. With just a squeeze of the bottle, Kewpie can help you achieve the perfect sear, give baked goods the right amount of fluff, and more. Here are five more reasons to reach for more Kewpie Mayonnaise.

1. Sub for yolks

If you're out of eggs when making carbonara or baking a cake, you can swap in Kewpie Mayonnaise to get the job done, since the condiment is made entirely with egg yolks. One tablespoon of mayonnaise roughly equals one egg yolk, or when measuring, you can squiggle out the size of a yolk as some Kewpie employees do. The mayonnaise also works well as an egg wash—just pat it evenly on whatever you're coating.

2. Show meat some TLC

It's well known among true Kewpie Mayonnaise fans that you can use the condiment to tenderize meat, whether that be meatballs or hunks of chicken. The emulsification of vinegar and oil is responsible for this. The acidity of the vinegar breaks down any tougher, fibrous bits while the oil gives the meat a soft, almost fluffy texture.

3. Emulsify more easily

Because it already has vinegar, fat, and egg yolks in it, Kewpie Mayonnaise is a great starting point for any salad dressing or sauce. You can lean into its creaminess with a Caesar-like dressing or introduce heat with a sprinkle of chili flakes or a bit of gochujang. Bonus: If your Kewpie bottle is almost empty (see page 64), mix everything together in the bottle itself, then taste and adjust to your liking.

4. Add a nice crust

There's a reason why any old mayonnaise can be used to create the perfect crust on a grilled cheese. The high amount of oil and egg in mayonnaise caramelize quickly and easily in a hot pan to add a nice char on the bread. But because Kewpie Mayonnaise has even more egg yolks than other mayos, you can go even further and create a deeper sear in other pan-fried dishes, too. Try it spread on sliced bread, cut vegetables, and even steak for nice browning and an extra roast-y flavor.

5. Level up baked goods

Kewpie Mayonnaise not only meets any baked good batter halfway, but it also improves upon whatever cake, flaky dough, or cookie you're making. The oil and eggs in Kewpie give cakes a moist and airy crumb and make pie, quiche, and galette doughs tender and wispy in all the right places. And don't worry: Your baked goods won't taste like mayonnaise.

Fish Roe Udon

Mentaiko pasta, spaghetti tossed in a rose-hued sauce mixed with tiny fish roe, is a classic example of wafu pasta, or Japanese-style pasta. This recipe plays with the form, giving it even more Japanese flair with the addition of thick udon noodles. They're the perfect vehicle for slurping up the creamy sauce enhanced with Kewpie mayo and pops of roe. You can find fish roe both fresh and frozen in Asian supermarkets. When making this dish, it's best to add the mayonnaise and fish roe once the pasta is off the heat. This way, the mayonnaise doesn't reduce and the fish roe maintains its fresh, vibrant flavor and look.

SERVES 2

- 3 tablespoons (45 g) unsalted butter
- 1 tablespoon finely chopped garlic
- 2 tablespoons sake
- 1 teaspoon hondashi (dashi powder) or salt
- 6 tablespoons (90 ml) Kewpie Mayonnaise
- ½ cup (120 ml) fish roe, such as tobiko or mentaiko
- 1 teaspoon lemon juice
- 2 blocks (400 g) fresh or frozen udon
- Kosher salt, as needed
- 2 tablespoons thinly sliced scallions
- 2 tablespoons furikake

1. Bring a large pot of water to a boil.
2. In a small saucepan, heat the butter over medium, until slightly browned. Turn the heat to low, add the garlic, cooking until fragrant, about 1 minute, and carefully add the sake and hondashi. Stir until dissolved and turn off the heat.
3. Whisk the mayonnaise into the pan to emulsify the sauce. Stir in ¼ cup (60 ml) fish roe and the lemon juice.
4. Cook the udon in the boiling water until it reaches your desired texture, and add the drained udon to the saucepan. Using tongs, toss the udon to coat with the sauce. Add salt as needed.
5. Serve the noodles on plates. Garnish each serving with the scallions, furikake, and remaining fish roe.

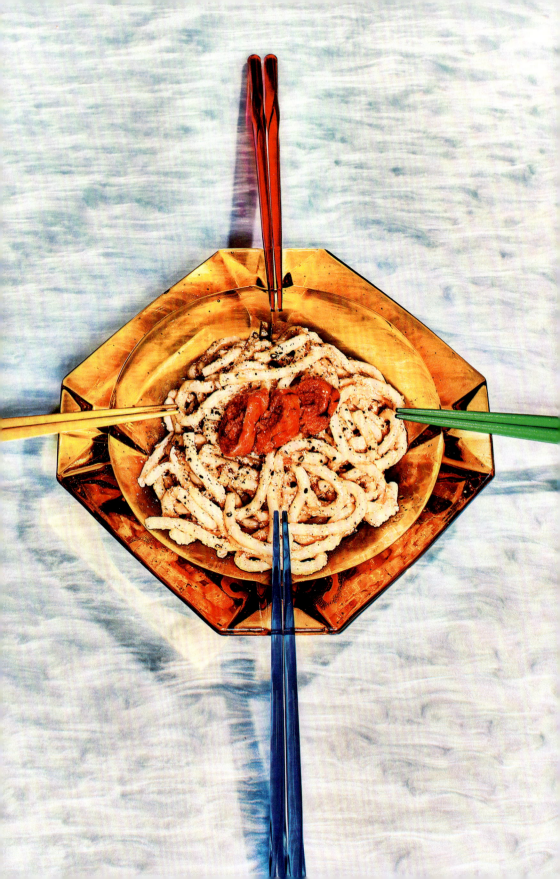

The

PEOPLE BEHIND KEWPIE MAYO

YOSHIMITSU MORI

CURRENT ROLE AT KEWPIE CORPORATION:
Senior adviser overseeing communications internally and externally

What was your first encounter with Kewpie Mayonnaise?
"I vividly remember my father used to put Kewpie Mayonnaise on white asparagus, probably canned, as a snack to go with his beer when I was little," he says. As a kid, Mori dismissed it as "grown-up food," so it wasn't until he was a university student that he tried the combination for himself. "I was amazed by the distinct umami and richness," he remembers.

Why did you want to work at the company?
"In my senior year of university and during my master's program, I conducted research focused on utilizing eggshells," Mori shares. He came across the numerous academic papers Kewpie had published on the subject of eggs, and he was impressed. "I found it to be a unique company, possessing both tradition and a pioneering spirit," he adds.

What's the most surprising thing you've learned about Kewpie Mayonnaise?
"I was deeply impressed by a quality-control manager at one of our suppliers, who once passionately explained to me just how special the salad oil used in Kewpie Mayonnaise is," he says. Mori got his start creating dressings in the R&D department and often met with suppliers, but this moment made him realize just how proud vendors are to work with them. The manager left a lasting impression on Mori: "I even began referring to this person as my 'Salad Oil Master.'"

How do you cook with Kewpie Mayonnaise at home?
"I believe Kewpie Mayonnaise is the best condiment for fried eggs, and I use it generously," he explains. Another one of Mori's house specialties is hamburg steak; he adds a bit of mayonnaise to the patty to make it juicier. "One of Kewpie Mayonnaise's secret recipe tricks!" Mori says.

KEWPIE IN THE WORLD

THREE-MINUTE COOKING

Long before the era of sheet-pan dinners and one-pot wonders, Yuichi Nakashima, the former chairman and the son of founder Toichiro Nakashima, wondered how he could help busy Japanese people make simple yet nutritious meals. His idea: a daily cooking demo on public television that showed how to cook one dish, such as shrimp croquettes or brothy miso oyster nabe, from scratch in just a few minutes. Some recipes didn't even feature Kewpie products, as Nakashima wanted to foster a love of home cooking rather than promote the company. *Three-Minute Cooking* debuted in 1962, notably a year before Julia Child's *The French Chef*. It became a fixture among Japanese viewers and is still airing, though today an episode can run as long as seven minutes.

In the kitchen with cooking instructor Kazuhide Miyamoto and TV host Akiko Tada in the 1980s

KEWPIE BY THE DECADE: The 1980s

By this time, Kewpie Mayonnaise had already become an everyday essential in Japanese home kitchens—and some American ones as well. Somehow, bottles of the mayo had arrived in the United States in the previous decade without the company's direct instruction. In response, Kewpie decided to seize the unexpected opportunity: In 1982, the company established its first overseas manufacturing facility, Q&B Foods in Los Angeles. (Read the full story of Kewpie's big American adventure on page 3.)

Meanwhile, in Japan, Kewpie chugged along, dialing in the details of its mayonnaise-making process. Mayonnaise production plants were already using egg-cracking machines that could break 300 eggs per minute, but Kewpie needed more to keep up with demand. So the company designed the QP-N600, which could crack up to, you guessed it, 600 eggs per minute. (Mayo fans can see the machine in action at Mayoterrace, the company's museum in Tokyo.)

Kewpie also adapted to the ebb and flow of Japanese society. With the rise of diet culture, the company began creating lower-calorie mayonnaises (see page 105), with some success. And as more women entered the workforce and the average family size shrunk in Japan, Kewpie anticipated the need for quick, ready-to-cook food offerings. It started developing its own in the form of canned salads and pasta sauce pouches, the latter featuring Kewpie's signature red mesh pattern.

Kewpie persisted in pursuing solutions to an issue that had plagued the company since the 1930s: what to do with all those egg whites. The company started its own Fine Chemicals Project Team to research its leftovers and find new ways to use them; it then created the Fine Chemicals Business to extract valuable elements from the egg whites that could be sold to pharmaceutical companies, such as lysozyme, which is often used in treating infections. Nakashima would have been proud.

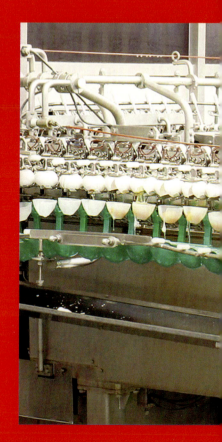

KEWPIE EXPANDS AT HOME—AND ABROAD

The QP-N600, Kewpie's specially designed egg breaking machine, in action!

Instantly Creamy Ramen

Want a bowl of velvety, thick instant noodles without any cheese or cream? Look no further than this ramen hack. All you need to do is whisk Kewpie Mayonnaise with the starchy noodle water to create a creamy sauce in a flash. Jazz it up with a jammy egg, a seasoning packet spiked with grated garlic, thinly sliced scallions, and a spoonful of chili crisp—or top it with whatever you have on hand. This recipe is made for solo slurping, but it's easy to scale up to feed a hungry crowd in just a few minutes.

SERVES 1

- 2 eggs, rinsed
- 1 pack instant ramen noodles, any brand with a seasoning packet
- 1 tablespoon Kewpie Mayonnaise
- 1 teaspoon minced garlic
- ½ teaspoon toasted sesame seeds
- 1 tablespoon thinly sliced scallions
- 1 teaspoon chili crisp

1. Bring 2½ cups (600 ml) of water to a boil in a medium-sized pot. Add 1 egg and cook for 7 minutes. Remove the jammy egg, peel, and set aside. Add the ramen noodles to the pot and cook, according to the package instructions, around 3 minutes.

2. While the egg and the noodles are cooking, add the mayonnaise, garlic, 1 cracked egg, and seasoning packet to a large soup bowl. Whisk well to combine.

3. Add about ¼ cup (60 ml) of ramen water to the mayonnaise mixture and whisk to combine. Then add the remaining ramen water and cooked ramen noodles. Stir until the sauce is creamy and evenly coats the noodles.

4. Slice the jammy egg in half and place it on the noodles. Sprinkle with the sesame seeds and scallions, and drizzle with the chili crisp. Serve immediately.

Yakisoba

This Japanese stir-fried noodle dish is a cousin of okonomiyaki, and it carries that familial trait of being quick to whip up and loaded with protein and vegetables. To ensure a nice char, it's important to cook the noodles, chicken thighs, and vegetables in batches which will prevent any steaming that happens as the result of an overcrowded pan. While you can buy yakisoba sauce, it's easy to make and doing so allows you to find the right balance of smoky, sweet, and savory. A final zigzag of Kewpie is essential to rounding out the flavors with a tangy, creamy note—just like with okonomiyaki.

SERVES 2

- 2 tablespoons ketchup
- 1 tablespoon oyster sauce
- 1 tablespoon Worcestershire sauce
- 1 tablespoon soy sauce
- 10 ounces (280 g) fresh yakisoba noodles
- 3 tablespoons (45 ml) neutral vegetable oil, such as canola
- 8 ounces (225 g) boneless, skinless chicken thighs, cut into ¼-inch (6 mm) strips
- 1 cup (52 g) thinly sliced cabbage
- ½ cup (26 g) thinly sliced yellow onions
- ½ teaspoon kosher salt
- ½ teaspoon freshly ground black pepper
- Kewpie Mayonnaise, for serving
- Aonori (nori flakes), for serving
- Benishoga (red pickled ginger), for serving

1. Make the yakisoba sauce: In a small bowl, stir together the ketchup, oyster sauce, Worcestershire sauce, and soy sauce until smooth. Set aside.

2. Boil the noodles for 1 minute less than indicated in the package directions. Drain and rinse with cold water while agitating with your hand to remove excess starch. When the water runs clear, drain well and shake off excess water. Place the noodles in a medium bowl and toss with 1 tablespoon vegetable oil to coat evenly.

3. Heat a large frying pan over high heat. Add the remaining vegetable oil and chicken and stir-fry until the chicken starts to brown around the edges, 2 to 3 minutes.

4. Add the cabbage, onions, salt, and black pepper. Stir-fry until the vegetables are slightly charred, 2 to 4 minutes. Add the noodles to the pan and stir-fry to reheat them.

5. Pour the yakisoba sauce over the noodles and toss to distribute evenly. Continue stir-frying for 1 to 2 minutes, allowing the sauce to caramelize slightly and become fragrant.

6. Serve on individual plates or family style. Drizzle mayonnaise over the noodles, sprinkle with aonori, and serve with a side of benishoga. Enjoy immediately.

Carbonara

This very simple (and very delicious) Roman pasta relies on the emulsification of cheese, raw egg yolks, and pasta and its water. Therein lies the tricky part of this dish: The cool yolks can easily scramble or clump together when added to the hot pasta. The solution is Kewpie Mayonnaise, which can substitute for some of the yolks because one tablespoon of Kewpie Mayonnaise is equal to one egg yolk. Adding a couple of tablespoons of Kewpie to the whole eggs will ensure the sauce (and your cooking fortitude) doesn't break.

SERVES 2

2 large eggs

2 tablespoons Kewpie Mayonnaise

1 cup (100 g) finely grated Parmesan or Pecorino, plus more for serving

1 teaspoon freshly ground black pepper, plus more as needed

1 tablespoon kosher salt, plus more as needed

8 ounces (225 g) spaghetti

6 ounces (175 g) pancetta or block bacon, cut into ¼-inch (6 mm) batons

1 teaspoon minced garlic

1. In a large mixing bowl, whisk together the eggs and mayonnaise until smooth. Stir in the Parmesan and black pepper. Set aside.

2. Bring a large pot of water to boil. Add the salt and cook the spaghetti according to package instructions until al dente. Reserve 1 cup (240 ml) of pasta cooking water, then drain the pasta.

3. While the pasta cooks, heat a large pan over medium heat. Add the pancetta and cook, stirring occasionally, until golden and crisp, about 6 to 7 minutes. Add the garlic and cook for another 30 seconds, until fragrant.

4. Add the hot pasta to the pan and toss to coat in pancetta fat. Transfer the pasta and any residual fat in the pan into the bowl with the egg mixture. Add ⅓ cup (80 ml) of pasta cooking water. Stir vigorously using chopsticks or tongs, until the pasta is coated with creamy sauce. If the mixture looks dry, add more pasta water, 1 tablespoon at a time, until the desired consistency is achieved. Season with salt and black pepper, as needed.

5. Divide the pasta onto serving plates or serve family-style, garnished with additional Parmesan and a generous sprinkle of ground black pepper. Eat while still hot.

MORE *than* MAYONNAISE

Kewpie isn't a one-hit wonder. Here's a snapshot of some of the company's most innovative products, past and present.

PRESERVED FRUIT

These were the canned fruit offerings of Aohata Canning, which initially focused on producing Nakashima's precious orange marmalade. In 1973, the company expanded to procuring, peeling, and packaging high-quality mandarins, white peaches, muscat, loquat, and other fruit. Today, Aohata has returned to its roots, making jams, savory spreads like chicken liver and oyster paste, and, of course, orange marmalade.

SALAD DRESSINGS

Starting in 1958, Kewpie began manufacturing Japan's first salad dressing, after employees came across the product in the U.S. Later, the company collaborated with the American brand Bernstein's to develop Western flavors, such as Thousand Island. Kewpie also invented the first Japanese oil-free salad dressing. Sold under the Janef brand, these low-calorie dressings were created to promote a healthy diet.

LIQUID EGGS

In 1977, Kewpie established the Kewpie Egg Corporation to expand production and distribution of liquid eggs. They were frozen and stored in containers that resemble old-school milk cartons. The timeless design, with its easy open-close spout, seemed to anticipate that liquid eggs would eventually become a staple in home kitchens, much like milk, and that prediction proved correct—it's now a multibillion-dollar industry worldwide!

MAYO EXPERIMENTS

In 1980, Kewpie Mayonnaise (American) hit the market. Contrary to what the name suggests, this mayonnaise wasn't made in America or even for American consumers. Rather, it was created to offer Japanese customers a lighter option made in the style of American mayonnaise, which was marked by a milder flavor thanks to its use of whole eggs rather than yolks. Two years after Kewpie Mayonnaise (American) came two more low-calorie, low-cholesterol products: Kewpie High Linoleic-Acid Dressing and Kewpie Light Caloric Dressing. However, the most successful version of these health-minded experiments was Kewpie Half, which launched in 1991 and boasted the full, rich taste of the original mayonnaise with half the calories.

Kewpie's primary products back in 1997, ranging from salad dressings to multiple (multiple!) types of mayonnaises

Spaghetti and Meatballs

It's hard to improve on a classic, but Kewpie may be your new favorite shortcut to creating moist and flavorful meatballs. The vinegar in it lightly tenderizes the meat while the emulsified oil helps maintain juiciness, and the condiment also keeps all the ingredients together. When these meatballs are popped into the oven they get a nice caramelized sheen, again thanks to the mayonnaise.

SERVES 6

- ¼ cup (60 ml) extra-virgin olive oil, plus more as needed
- 6 tablespoons (90 g) chopped garlic
- 3 tablespoons plus 1½ teaspoons kosher salt, plus more as needed
- 2½ teaspoons freshly ground black pepper, plus more as needed
- Two 28-ounce (795 g) cans tomato passata or tomato puree
- 1 teaspoon dried oregano
- 3 tablespoons (45 ml) whole milk
- ⅓ cup (55 g) panko bread crumbs
- 1 large egg
- ¼ cup (60 ml) Kewpie Mayonnaise
- ½ cup (50 g) finely grated Parmesan or Pecorino, plus more for serving
- 1 pound (450 g) 80% lean/20% fat ground beef
- 8 ounces (225 g) ground pork
- ¼ cup (25 g) coarsely grated yellow onion
- 2 tablespoons finely chopped fresh parsley, plus more for serving
- 1 pound (450 g) spaghetti

1. Make the sauce: Heat the olive oil in a medium Dutch oven or heavy pot over medium. Add 3 tablespoons garlic, 2 tablespoons salt, and 2 teaspoons black pepper. Cook, stirring, until fragrant, about 10 to 20 seconds. Add the tomato passata and oregano. Add ¼ cup (60 ml) of water to each can, swirl, and pour into the pot. Stir and bring to a simmer. Reduce heat to low, partially cover, and simmer gently for 15 to 20 minutes, until the sauce slightly thickens. Cover and keep warm.

2. Preheat the oven to 450°F (230°C) and line two baking sheets with parchment paper.

3. Make the meatballs: In a large bowl, mix the whole milk, panko, egg, mayonnaise, Parmesan, 3 tablespoons garlic, 1½ teaspoons salt, and ½ teaspoon black pepper with a fork. Add the ground beef, ground pork, onion, and parsley. Gently mix with a spatula until fully incorporated, being careful not to overwork the mixture.

4. Using a #24 ice cream scoop (about 3 tablespoons/ 45 ml), portion the meat mixture into approximately 18 meatballs. Arrange the meatballs on the prepared baking sheets and shape them with oiled hands. Bake on the bottom rack for 8 to 9 minutes, until browned and sizzling.

5. Transfer the meatballs and any juices to the simmering sauce. Stir gently and cook for 3 to 4 minutes, until the meatballs are cooked through and the flavors meld. Season with additional salt and black pepper, as needed.

6. Meanwhile, bring a large pot of water to a boil with 1 tablespoon salt. Cook the spaghetti according to package directions until al dente. Drain the pasta. Return the pasta to the pot and toss with 2 cups (480 ml) of sauce.

7. Divide the pasta among serving bowls, top with the meatballs and remaining sauce, and garnish with additional parsley and Parmesan. Serve immediately.

Baked Mac and Cheese

The best part of this mac and cheese isn't the intense cheesy flavor, nor the crown of crunchy panko. It's the fact that you don't need to make a finicky roux to get a textbook velvety smooth sauce. All you need is some Kewpie Mayonnaise and sour cream. They do the heavy lifting of binding everything, so the mac and cheese isn't loose and soupy but thick and caramelized. Even better: You can make the dish ahead of time, so hot mac and cheese is ready as a festive main or dinner party side whenever you need it.

SERVES 8

Cooking spray or 1 teaspoon neutral vegetable oil, such as canola

Kosher salt

8 ounces (225 g) elbow macaroni

8 ounces (225 g) grated Monterey Jack

8 ounces (225 g) grated sharp Cheddar

1 cup (240 ml) Kewpie Mayonnaise, room temperature

1 cup (240 ml) full-fat sour cream, room temperature

¾ cup (90 g) panko bread crumbs

2 tablespoons salted butter, melted

¼ teaspoon garlic powder

Chopped fresh parsley, for serving

Paprika, for serving

1. Preheat the oven to 350°F (180°C). Grease a 2-quart (1.9 L) baking dish and set aside.

2. Cook the macaroni in a large pot of well-salted boiling water according to package directions for al dente. The pasta should still be a little bit firm, since it will continue to cook in the oven. Drain the pasta, then return to the pot.

3. Stir in the Monterey Jack, Cheddar, mayonnaise, and sour cream. Mix until completely combined. Transfer the pasta mixture to the prepared baking dish.

4. Make the panko topping: In a small pan, stir together the panko, butter, and garlic powder. Toast over medium-low heat, stirring constantly, until golden brown.

5. Bake the pasta, uncovered, for 15 to 20 minutes, or until the filling is hot and bubbly and the top is lightly browned.

6. Sprinkle the panko topping on top of the pasta, and garnish with parsley and paprika. Serve immediately.

7. The mac and cheese can be made 3 days in advance, stored in the refrigerator without the panko topping. (The topping can also be prepped ahead of time—keep it in an airtight container at room temperature for up to a week.) When you're ready to bake, sprinkle the panko on top of the mac and cheese before sliding the dish into the oven.

豆腐　魚介類　肉類

tofu　seafood　meat

TAMAGO SANDO 116

KATSU SANDO 117

GRILLED CHEESE 121

SHRIMP BURGERS 122

CHEESEBURGERS 129

OKONOMIYAKI 131

FISH TACOS 132

FRITTO MISTO with TARTAR SAUCE 135

HONEY-WALNUT SHRIMP 136

CRISPY TOFU with SCALLION-GINGER SAUCE 139

KARAAGE 140

HOT HONEY BABY BACK RIBS 143

KEWPIE BY THE DECADE

The 1990s & 2000s

Nakashima, Kewpie's founder, always stuck to his guns, and in the midst of constant change during the turn of the century, Kewpie Corporation followed suit. When Japan's bubble economy in the 1990s began to burst, leading to a 25 percent reduction in income for many people, Kewpie decided to lower prices to better fit consumers' pocketbooks. This wasn't the first time Kewpie made such a decision; over the tenure of his chairmanship, Nakashima repeatedly reduced the cost of mayonnaise so that Kewpie Mayonnaise could remain a daily essential for all, even through tough times.

Still Kewpie had to adapt to the times. Throughout this time Kewpie dabbled in new food products, from baby food (Kewpie Gourmet Baby) to easy-to-digest meals for the elderly (Janef Nursing Care Food). Some took off, while others didn't—and you can see some of those experiments, which of course includes mayonnaise, below.

In the early years of Kewpie, Nakashima famously stated, "I prefer to not make a large company."

One Kewpie innovation: Its line of hearty (and simple to prepare) food for elderly people

KEWPIE ADAPTS

But more than seventy years after its founding, Kewpie was no longer a small family business but an industry leader employing thousands of people and creating seemingly endless products. (In 2025, one hundred years after the launch of Kewpie Mayonnaise, the company has grown to over ten thousand employees in Japan and the United States.) To help different departments connect and understand one another, Kewpie started its own in-house trade fair in 2005. Over seven hundred employees set up stations, complete with tastings and intricate panels, to share their processes and products. It was so successful that Kewpie has made these fairs and similarly collaborative events a regular occurrence.

Despite the size of these gatherings, Nakashima would have certainly liked them as well. They speak to another aspiration he had for his company: everyone working together to achieve the common goal of making something special.

Some early packaging designs as Kewpie entered the world of baby food (left) and high-end salad dressings (right)

Tamago Sando

What makes a Japanese-style egg sandwich so delicious and distinct from other variations is the eggs and the mayonnaise. It requires two types of boiled eggs: a hard-boiled 12-minute egg to mash up with mayonnaise and other seasonings, as well as a jammier 7-minute egg to go in the center of the sandwich. Together, they make for one luscious egg salad. The mayonnaise, of course, is Kewpie, which is esteemed for its light creaminess and umami-packed flavor. In this recipe, we up the umami factor by adding hondashi (or dashi in powder form) to the mayonnaise, bringing out the savory side of Kewpie Mayonnaise. Tamago sando is perfect for a light lunch or picnics and can be made ahead of time.

SERVES 2

5 large eggs

3 tablespoons (45 ml) Kewpie Mayonnaise

2 teaspoons Dijon mustard

1 teaspoon honey

½ teaspoon hondashi (dashi powder) or bouillon powder

4 slices shokupan (Japanese milk bread)

1 teaspoon thinly sliced fresh chives (optional)

1. Prepare a large bowl with ice water.

2. In a large pot, add enough water to cover all the eggs by at least 1 inch (2 cm). Bring to a boil and carefully drop in the eggs, maintaining a gentle boil. At the 7-minute mark, take one egg out and plunge it into the ice water. At the 12-minute mark, take out the rest of the eggs and plunge them into ice water. Let the eggs chill in the bowl for at least 5 minutes.

3. Crack and peel all the eggs. Cut the 7-minute egg in half lengthwise and set it aside.

4. Cut the remaining eggs in half lengthwise and remove the yolks from the whites. Place the egg yolks in a bowl and mash them with a fork. Then, roughly chop the egg whites and add them to the mashed egg yolks. Add the mayonnaise, Dijon mustard, honey, and hondashi to the bowl and mix well.

5. On a slice of bread, evenly spread a quarter of the egg salad mixture. Then, place one half of the 7-minute egg, yolk side down, in the middle. Top it with another quarter of the egg salad mixture and spread it as evenly as possible. Place another slice of bread on top and press gently. Repeat with the other sandwich.

6. Serve the tamago sando cut in half and garnish with the chives if desired. If preparing in advance, wrap the sandwich, cut or uncut, in parchment paper and keep in the refrigerator for up to 8 hours.

Katsu Sando

This isn't the typical katsu sando sold in Japanese convenience stores. Between the breaded-and-fried pork chops, fluffy milk bread, and generous dose of smoky-sweet tonkatsu sauce is the nontraditional addition of a spicy slaw. This tangle of cabbage, which is dressed with Kewpie Mayonnaise and yuzu kosho (a citrusy pepper paste), balances out all the fatty, crunchy elements of the sandwich. If you don't have yuzu kosho on hand, you can substitute lemon zest mixed with your hot sauce of choice to still get that hit of tangy heat.

MAKES 4 SANDWICHES

- 4 garlic cloves, finely grated
- ¾ cup (180 ml) Kewpie Mayonnaise
- 2 teaspoons yuzu kosho
- ¼ medium head green cabbage (about 12 ounces/340 g), cored and thinly sliced
- 2 medium scallions, thinly sliced
- 4 boneless pork chops (1-inch/2 cm thick, 5 to 6 ounces/140 to 170 g each)
- 1 teaspoon kosher salt, plus more as needed
- 1 cup (125 g) all-purpose flour
- 2 large eggs, whisked
- 1 cup (100 g) panko bread crumbs
- Neutral vegetable oil, such as canola, for frying
- 8 slices shokupan (Japanese milk bread) or white sandwich bread, ½-inch-thick (12 mm)
- ½ cup (120 ml) tonkatsu sauce

1. Make the cabbage slaw: In a large bowl, combine the garlic, ½ cup (120 ml) mayonnaise, and yuzu kosho. Add the cabbage and scallions, and toss until evenly coated. Set aside.

2. Place each pork chop on a cutting board and use a meat mallet or the bottom of a small pan to pound into ½-inch (12 mm) thickness. Season both sides with the salt.

3. Prepare the dredging stations: Place the flour, eggs, and panko in three separate shallow bowls.

4. Dredge each chop in the flour, shaking off the excess, then coat in the eggs, and cover with panko. Place the breaded pork chops on a baking sheet.

5. Place a wire rack over another baking sheet and set aside.

6. In a Dutch oven or high-sided skillet, heat enough oil to reach about 2 inches (5 cm) on the side of the pot, over medium-high heat until it reaches 350°F (180°C). Fry each pork chop individually until golden brown on both sides and cooked through, about 3 to 5 minutes total. Transfer to the wire rack, and lightly season with salt as needed.

7. Assemble the sandwiches: Lay out the bread slices. Spread 1 tablespoon mayonnaise on four slices of bread, and spread 2 tablespoons tonkatsu sauce on the remaining four slices. Place a pork chop on each of the bread slices that have tonkatsu sauce, and portion the cabbage slaw evenly over each pork chop. Top with the mayonnaise-spread bread slices, mayonnaise side down.

8. Trim the sandwich edges for a clean presentation, and then cut each sandwich in half to form two rectangles, wiping the knife between cuts for cleaner edges. Enjoy immediately.

Tamago Sando, page 116

★ A DISH POWERED BY KEWPIE ★

No sandwich can match the star power of egg salad sandwiches sold at Japanese convenience stores. They're simple—hard-boiled eggs, bread, mayonnaise, salt, and pepper— but that's why they're so elusive to recreate. According to sandwich sleuths, the key is Kewpie Mayonnaise. Since tamago sando has few ingredients, each one counts—and Kewpie brings a luxurious creaminess and umami-packed flavor.

Katsū Sando, page 117

Grilled Cheese

Most sandwiches are defined by what goes between the two slices of bread, but what makes this grilled cheese so exceptional is what goes on the *outside*. Here, an easy spread of Kewpie Mayonnaise, Dijon mustard, and black pepper is slathered all over the bread before toasting in the pan. The exterior coating adds a whole new pop of flavor to the sandwich while also protecting it from burning in the pan, thanks to the high smoke point of the mayo. To take things one step further, sliced ripe tomato cuts through the richness of the sandwich and adds an extra layer of umami—feel free to omit it, though, if you're a grilled cheese purist.

SERVES 1

¼ cup (60 ml) Kewpie Mayonnaise

2 teaspoons Dijon mustard

1 teaspoon freshly ground black pepper

2 slices bread

2 slices Cheddar

2 thin slices (¼-inch/6 mm thick) beefsteak tomato

1. In a small bowl, mix the mayonnaise, Dijon mustard, and black pepper together. Spread 1 tablespoon of the mixture on both sides of each slice of bread.

2. Heat a small frying pan over medium-low. Place one slice of bread in the frying pan. Add a slice of Cheddar, followed by the tomato slices, and then top with another slice of cheese. (It's important that the tomato is thinly cut or it won't cook through.) Cover with the second slice of bread.

3. Cook the sandwich until the bottom side is golden brown and the cheese starts to melt, pressing it down occasionally, about 3 to 5 minutes. Carefully flip the sandwich and cook the other side until golden brown and the cheese is fully melted, 3 to 4 minutes.

4. Remove the sandwich from the pan, cut it in half diagonally, and serve immediately while it's hot and the cheese is still gooey.

Shrimp Burgers

This recipe is an ode to the popular shrimp cutlet burger at MOS Burger, Japan's beloved burger chain. It's a cult favorite for its crispy golden crust and meaty shrimp patty. This version doesn't mess with patty perfection, though it does riff on the burger accoutrements. Instead of the usual tartar sauce, the shrimp burger is topped with a Kewpie-powered egg salad plus a swipe of wasabi mayonnaise for a sneaky hit of heat. The shrimp patties come together quickly but can be made in advance, too.

SERVES 4

- 4 hard-boiled eggs, coarsely chopped
- ¼ medium onion, finely chopped
- ¼ cup (60 ml) Kewpie Mayonnaise
- 2 tablespoons ketchup
- 1 teaspoon kosher salt, plus more as needed
- 12 ounces (340 g) shrimp, peeled and deveined
- 2 teaspoons potato starch or cornstarch
- ½ teaspoon freshly ground black pepper
- 2 large eggs, beaten
- Neutral vegetable oil, such as canola, for frying
- 1 cup (100 g) panko bread crumbs
- ⅓ cup (45 g) all-purpose flour
- 2 tablespoons unsalted butter
- 4 brioche buns, split
- ¼ cup (60 ml) wasabi mayonnaise, store bought or homemade
- ¼ medium head savoy cabbage (about 12 ounces/340 g), cored and thinly sliced

1. Make the egg salad: Mix the hard-boiled eggs, onion, mayonnaise, ketchup, and ½ teaspoon salt in a small bowl until combined. Set aside.

2. Cut one-third of the shrimp into ½-inch (12 mm) pieces; finely chop the remaining shrimp (or pulse in a food processor). Transfer all shrimp to a medium bowl. Mix in the potato starch, black pepper, 1 tablespoon beaten eggs, and remaining salt. Using oiled hands, divide the mixture into 4 portions, then shape into ½-inch-thick (12 mm) patties. Place on an oiled baking sheet and chill in the refrigerator for at least 1 hour and up to 12.

3. Place the panko, flour, and remaining beaten eggs in 3 separate shallow bowls. Working with one patty at a time, dredge in flour, shaking off excess. Dip in eggs, letting excess drip back into the bowl, then coat in panko, pressing to adhere before shaking off excess.

4. Pour the oil into a large cast-iron skillet or Dutch oven, to come 1 inch (2 cm) up the side. Heat the oil over medium until the thermometer registers 350°F (180°C).

5. Working in two batches, carefully slide patties into the oil and fry, turning halfway through, until golden brown and cooked through, about 3 minutes per side. Transfer to a wire rack set inside a rimmed baking sheet; season with salt.

6. Melt 1 tablespoon butter in another large skillet over medium heat. Working in two batches and adding the remaining butter between batches, toast the buns, cut sides down, until golden brown, about 2 minutes. Transfer to plates.

7. Spread each bottom bun with 1 tablespoon wasabi mayonnaise. Top each with some cabbage and a patty. Spoon the reserved egg salad over and close the burgers. Serve immediately.

How KEWPIE MAYO Went WORLDWIDE

(Spoiler alert: It involves a mayonnaise black market, a secret mission, and TikTok.)

The Earth is billions of years old, and still there are some mysteries we humans have not yet solved. Who built Stonehenge, and how did they do it? Was it always spelled *The Berenstain Bears*? (Not *-stein*?!) How, in the 1970s, did Kewpie Mayonnaise end up in the aisles of American grocery stores unbeknownst to the company? Well, we have a better sense of that last one.

For the first fifty-plus years of Kewpie's existence, it was a virtual unknown in the States. In Japan, it was the bestselling domestic mayonnaise and, as a result, a fixture in pretty much every home cook's kitchen. After World War II, Kewpie Mayonnaise had reached the same level of popularity as miso, soy sauce, and rice. It had been grafted onto the Japanese culinary canon, so normalized that it was almost an afterthought. And it was that quiet ubiquity that ultimately led to Kewpie's big adventure to America.

During the 1960s and '70s, Japanese ingredients were gaining traction in foreign countries, and somehow during this time, Kewpie found its way onto the shelves of Japanese grocery stores and regional supermarkets in the United States. How Kewpie embarked on its maiden voyage remains a mystery, but a likely theory is that Japanese distributors began sending out any and all products they could get their hands on—even if the producers hadn't officially signed on to sell overseas.

By the mid-1970s, word came back to corporate that Kewpie mayo had inadvertently made its way to the other side of the world. While it was great news that a love for Kewpie was growing in America, without control of the distribution, there was no way to regulate the quality or authenticity of the product. Was the mayo imported with care for the integrity of the package and ingredients? Were customers enjoying fresh Kewpie mayo or were the American shelves stacked with expired products? Was it even real Kewpie at all? In 1976, Kewpie dispatched a representative from Japan to do some condiment reconnaissance in America. His job would be to check the condition and shelf life of the mayonnaise and then establish a legitimate distribution channel to properly export Kewpie Mayonnaise.

It took three years for Kewpie's man on the ground to complete his mission. While he searched for and ultimately secured a U.S. importing partner, he noticed just how big the American mayonnaise market was. Even in a crowded field with power players like Best Foods and Hellmann's, Kewpie's representative felt that the Japanese mayonnaise would be appreciated in America just as much as in Japan.

When he filed his report to Kewpie HQ, he proposed a wild idea: The company shouldn't just export its mayonnaise to America; it should start *manufacturing* its mayonnaise there. His reasoning was that it would be more cost-effective, allowing the company to more competitively price its product and produce a fresher mayonnaise with a longer shelf life. Kewpie agreed and gave the green light. In 1982, he opened up the American branch of Kewpie called Q&B Foods.

Kewpie's launch in America marked a new era for the company. In many ways, it was a full-circle moment, achieving the original mission of the founder. As one Kewpie employee puts it, "Mr. Toichiro Nakashima encountered mayonnaise when he was in the U.S. in the 1910s. After that, he put his energy in Japan for almost fifty years. So it would be kind of like an encouragement for Kewpie to see the mayonnaise we've been making, we've been distributing, to be accepted in the U.S. market."

In 1982, Q&B Foods converted a 710-square-foot warehouse in Baldwin Park, just east of Los Angeles, into its first overseas office and manufacturing plant. As a new company making a product new to American suppliers, it took time to connect with vendors and procure raw materials. As such, for three decades Q&B Foods methodically built out its American arsenal of products and manufactured mayonnaise for Japanese restaurants and imported Kewpie Mayonnaise for retail. Behind the scenes, Q&B experimented with the mayonnaise recipe with the aim of creating a Kewpie Mayonnaise for every American customer, no matter their taste preference. In addition to the signature yolk-only version (known as Red at the company), it developed a whole-egg version (Blue). A separate challenge was recreating the same soft, squeezable bottle used in Japan. To fit in with other American mayos on the shelves, Kewpie opted for a firmer plastic bottle and wrapped its label directly on it.

Finally, in 2016, Q&B Foods's Kewpie Mayonnaise made its official debut in the mayonnaise aisles of America. In the beginning, sales lagged among the general public, but the condiment became a cult ingredient among food industry insiders. Chefs sang its praises, reaching for no other mayo in deviled eggs, karaage, and more, and dubbed it as "the king of mayonnaise." Reputable food publications like *Bon Appétit* and *Food52* conducted mayonnaise taste tests and described Kewpie as "the most eggy" and "a happy mayo," often proclaiming Kewpie a top-tier pick.

Soon big grocery chains and retail markets started to catch on. Not long after its official launch in America, they approached Q&B Foods, hoping to sell Kewpie Mayonnaise. Attention from these food industry giants certainly seemed promising, but with American sales still mostly limited to culinary professionals, who knew if everyone else was ready for Kewpie Mayonnaise?

At this point, you know that trepidation isn't in Kewpie's DNA. After all, Nakashima created his own recipe for the American condiment and introduced it to Japan when a market for it didn't exist, simply because he loved it. So the company took the risk—and never looked back. Sales were better than expected: "It was proof that Japanese mayonnaise was accepted by American consumers," according to the employee.

However, in the twenty-first century, success isn't measured just by SKUs but also by social media dominance. Since the dawn of mini cooking demos on platforms like Instagram, TikTok, and YouTube, content creators have been reaching for Kewpie Mayonnaise to finish okonomiyaki, add instant creaminess to instant noodles, and more.

But Kewpie's popularity skyrocketed during COVID as much of the world was stuck at home with time to scroll and to cook. Many people were searching for Kewpie mayo—"You could see Kewpie getting bigger and bigger on Google Trends," says another Kewpie employee—and it became the star of viral dishes that came to define this era of comforting cooking. One such post came in 2021 from a popular content creator, Emily Mariko, whose recipe for a simple meal of microwaved salmon and rice drizzled with Kewpie Mayonnaise became a TikTok sensation. Google search trends for the condiment quadrupled and some retailers reportedly sold out. Social media confirmed what Q&B Foods had hoped for all along when it first started manufacturing mayonnaise on American soil: Its Japanese mayonnaise had finally caught on.

Now, after a few decades in America, Kewpie Mayonnaise has become an essential ingredient in American kitchens and beyond. In 2024 alone, Q&B Foods sold four million bottles in the United States. "Who'd have thought a condiment would reach celebrity status?" *The Independent* wrote of Kewpie Mayonnaise in 2021. In that open-ended question is the answer to Kewpie's surprising yet snowballing success: Mystery is, and forever will be, the secret sauce.

KEWPIE IN THE WORLD

MAYONNAISE CLASS

Did you know you can get an education in all things Kewpie Mayonnaise? The company launched interactive mayonnaise workshops at Japanese elementary schools in 2002. Young students learn the science and nutrition of Kewpie Mayonnaise by making their own batch, which they then enjoy with cut vegetables. Mayonnaise Class is led by Kewpie employees who are "Mayo Star" certified, meaning they've passed an in-house exam that equips them to teach elementary students all about mayonnaise. And being a Mayo Star is an esteemed rank—there are many applicants but fewer than 300 make the cut. So far, Mayonnaise Class has reached more than 100,000 students in some 2,000 schools. After attending a Mayonnaise Class in 2019, one fifth-grader in Japan declared, "I was able to eat cucumbers for the first time, even though I hated them. It was surprisingly tasty."

A Mayo-Star-certified Kewpie employee showing students the ropes of mayonnaise-making

Cheeseburgers

The all-American cheeseburger needs no introduction, but this variation does have a secret technique hidden in the patty. Kewpie is mixed into the ground beef to tenderize and flavor the meat, and it also melds everything together so that you can form thin, quick-cooking patties. Top it with your choice of cheese and the usual lettuce, tomato, onions, and pickles, but don't forget an extra smear of Kewpie Mayonnaise on the bun.

SERVES 4

- 1 pound (450 g) 80-85% lean/15-20% fat ground beef
- ¼ cup (60 ml) Kewpie Mayonnaise, plus more for serving
- 1 teaspoon kosher salt
- 1 teaspoon freshly ground black pepper
- 1 teaspoon vegetable oil
- 4 slices American or Cheddar cheese
- Four 3-inch slider buns, toasted
- Ketchup
- Torn lettuce leaves
- Sliced red onion
- Sliced pickles

1. Place the ground beef and mayonnaise in a medium mixing bowl and sprinkle with the salt and black pepper. Mix gently to combine.

2. Divide the meat into four equal portions, then roll each portion into a ball. Place one ball on a baking sheet and gently press it into a ½-inch-thick (12 mm), round patty. With your thumb, press a "moat" approximately ¼ to ½ inch (0.6 to 1.25 cm) from the edge, around the circumference of the burger. The edge should be slightly higher than the indentation to ensure the burger flattens evenly while cooking. Repeat this process with the remaining portions.

3. Heat the oil in a large skillet over medium heat. When the pan is hot, carefully place the patties in the skillet, leaving some space between each patty.

4. Cook the burgers until nicely seared and browned halfway up the sides, about 2 to 3 minutes.

5. Flip the burgers and cook the patties 2 to 3 more minutes. Turn off the heat and place the cheese atop the patties; cover the skillet with a lid for 1 to 2 minutes, until the cheese melts.

6. Serve the burgers on the buns spread with mayonnaise and ketchup and layered with lettuce, tomato, red onion, and pickles. Enjoy right away.

★ **A DISH POWERED BY KEWPIE** ★

A crosshatched drizzle of Kewpie Mayonnaise is a signature of this savory Japanese pancake. Okonomiyaki translates to "what/how you like grilled," which means anything goes, including Kewpie. Its buttery tang complements all the salty, fishy, and vegetal flavors of the griddled pancake, from the protein and cabbage inside to the fluttering katsuobushi on top.

Okonomiyaki

The golden rule of okonomiyaki is *don't touch it*. Once you stir together the batter and pour it on a hot pan, it's easy to poke and prod at the pancake to see if it's ready to flip. This, however, disturbs the pancake from cooking evenly. Let your senses tell you when it's ready—you should smell a lightly toasty scent and see the pancake looking less runny and a little firmer. (If you end up undercooking the okonomiyaki, you can always add it back to the hot pan and cover it for a couple of minutes.) And of course, no okonomiyaki is complete without squiggles of Kewpie Mayonnaise and okonomiyaki sauce and a fistful of aonori and katsuobushi on top.

MAKES 4 PANCAKES

- 4 slices bacon, sliced into 1-inch (2 cm) pieces
- 3 large eggs
- 1 teaspoon hondashi (dashi powder) dissolved in ½ cup (120 ml) water or any kind of stock
- 1 teaspoon kosher salt
- ⅔ cup (85 g) all-purpose flour
- 2 tablespoons cornstarch or potato starch
- ¼ medium head green cabbage (about 12 ounces/340 g), cored and finely shredded
- 1 to 2 scallions, sliced
- ½ cup (120 g) fresh or canned corn
- 4 tablespoons (60 ml) neutral vegetable oil, such as canola
- 2 tablespoons Kewpie Mayonnaise
- 2 tablespoons okonomiyaki sauce
- 1 teaspoon aonori (nori flakes)
- 1 teaspoon katsuobushi (bonito flakes)

1. In a large frying pan over medium heat, fry the bacon until cooked through and crispy, about 4 to 5 minutes. Set the bacon aside to cool. Pour out the fat for other uses and wipe the pan, reserving it for later.

2. In a medium bowl, combine the eggs, hondashi, and salt and beat gently. In a separate large mixing bowl, add the flour and cornstarch. Pour the egg mixture over the flour and stir the batter until smooth.

3. Add the cabbage, half of the scallions, cooked bacon, and corn into the batter. Mix gently until all the ingredients are evenly coated. If there's excess batter liquid at the bottom, add a little more shredded cabbage and mix through gently.

4. Heat the reserved large frying pan over medium heat and add 1 tablespoon oil. Scoop 1 cup (240 ml) of the mixture into the pan, shaping a circle about 4 inches (10 cm) wide. Cook one pancake at a time, 3 to 4 minutes per side without disturbing, and carefully flip with a fish spatula, until golden brown on both sides. Transfer your freshly cooked pancake to a serving plate. Wipe the pan and repeat with the rest of the mixture, adding 1 tablespoon oil in between each pancake.

5. Once all pancakes are cooked, drizzle each with the mayonnaise and okonomiyaki sauce. Sprinkle with the aonori and katsuobushi, and garnish with the remaining scallions. Serve right away.

Fish Tacos

These flaky, flavor-packed tacos use Kewpie Mayonnaise to its full potential. The mayo is the base for a creamy, zingy sauce, plus it acts as batter for the fish fillets. This dredge tenderizes the fish, creates a delicious coating, and protects it from the heat, essentially replacing an arsenal of ingredients typically used in a beer-battered fish. Better yet, no deep-fry is necessary to get that ideal fall-apart interior and craggy-crispy exterior. Load up each taco with big chunks of the fish, a pile of slaw, sliced avocados and radish, cilantro, and a mandatory spoonful of the leftover slaw sauce.

SERVES 4

- ½ cup (120 g) sour cream
- ¾ cup (180 ml) Kewpie Mayonnaise
- 2 tablespoons lime juice
- ¼ small head red cabbage (about 2 cups/ 180 g), cored and shredded
- 8 taco-sized corn or flour tortillas
- 2 teaspoons chipotle chili powder
- 1 teaspoon kosher salt
- 1 pound (450 g) cod, tilapia, halibut, or other whitefish fillets
- 1 avocado, sliced
- 4 breakfast radishes, thinly sliced
- ⅓ cup (15 g) fresh cilantro leaves
- 4 lime wedges, for serving

1. Make the slaw sauce: In a small bowl, combine the sour cream, ½ cup (120 ml) mayonnaise, and lime juice. Stir until combined.

2. Assemble the slaw: In a medium bowl, combine the cabbage with 2 tablespoons of the sauce. Stir to coat the cabbage with a thin layer of sauce. Place the remaining sauce aside.

3. In a dry skillet over medium-high heat, warm the tortillas one at a time for about 30 seconds on both sides. To keep the tortillas warm, stack and wrap them in a clean dish towel until serving.

4. In a small bowl, mix the remaining mayonnaise with the chipotle chili powder and salt. Gently rub this mixture onto the fish fillets to coat them.

5. Heat a nonstick skillet over medium heat. Add the fish to the pan and cook for 2 minutes. Flip the fish, reduce the heat to medium-low, and cook for another 3 to 4 minutes. The fish is done when it is opaque all the way through and breaks apart easily.

6. Transfer the cooked fillets to a bowl and use a fork or knife to gently break the fish into large chunks. Assemble the tacos with a few pieces of fish, some slaw, avocado, radish, cilantro, and a drizzle of the slaw sauce. Serve with the lime wedges.

Fritto Misto *with* Tartar Sauce

This Italian-style fried seafood is known for its crisp lightness, and in this globe-trotting riff, it's served with a pickle-heavy tartar sauce, the constant companion of fried foods in the United States. These two culinary inspirations combined make for an appetizer that hits all the right spots: It's crunchy, creamy, and flavorful. The puckery Kewpie tartar sauce also goes well with french fries, chicken nuggets, or whatever fried food your heart desires.

SERVES 4

- 1 cup (240 ml) Kewpie Mayonnaise
- 1 tablespoon finely chopped capers
- 1 tablespoon finely chopped fresh dill
- ¼ cup (35 g) finely chopped gherkins or dill pickles
- 1 tablespoon finely chopped red onion
- 1 tablespoon lemon juice
- 2 teaspoons freshly ground black pepper
- 1 teaspoon kosher salt, plus more as needed
- 1 cup (120 g) all-purpose flour
- ½ cup (60 g) potato starch or cornstarch
- Neutral vegetable oil, such as canola, for frying
- 1 pound (450 g) shrimp, peeled and deveined
- 5 ounces (150 g) calamari, cleaned and cut into ½-inch-thick (12 mm) pieces
- 7 ounces (200 g) whitefish, cut into ½-inch-thick (12 mm) pieces
- ½ teaspoon white pepper, plus more as needed
- ½ teaspoon powdered sugar, plus more as needed
- Lemon wedges, for serving
- Chopped fresh parsley, for serving

1. Make the tartar sauce: In a small bowl, combine the mayonnaise, capers, dill, gherkins, red onion, lemon juice, and 1 teaspoon black pepper. Stir well to combine. Season the tartar sauce with salt as needed. Set aside.
2. In a large bowl, whisk together the flour, potato starch, ½ teaspoon salt, and remaining black pepper.
3. Heat a pot over medium-high heat and add enough oil to reach about 2 inches (5 cm) on the side of the pot. Heat the oil to 375°F (190°C). Prepare a sheet pan lined with a wire rack for draining the fried seafood.
4. Coat the shrimp, calamari, and whitefish in the flour mixture, ensuring each piece is evenly coated. Dust off any excess flour, then fry the seafood in batches for 2 to 3 minutes, until golden brown and crispy. Remove from the oil with tongs and transfer to the wire rack for 1 minute to drain the excess oil.
5. Once drained, sprinkle the fried seafood with the remaining salt, white pepper, and powdered sugar. Toss gently to coat evenly. Adjust seasoning, as needed.
6. Serve the fried seafood on a platter with lemon wedges, parsley, and the tartar sauce for dipping.

Honey-Walnut Shrimp

It's impossible to *not* order this dish whenever you see it on the menu of a Chinese restaurant. Fans of honey-walnut shrimp will be happy to know it's straightforward to whip up at home, whether you're hosting a feast or satisfying a very specific craving. The best part of this classic banquet main is the signature sweet-sour, pearly sauce that is typically made with condensed milk and mayonnaise. Here Kewpie gives the definitive sauce an extra-luscious texture and savory punch.

SERVES 4

2 tablespoons granulated sugar

1 tablespoon honey

½ teaspoon kosher salt, plus more as needed

1 cup (120 g) toasted walnut halves, about 30

¼ cup (60 ml) Kewpie Mayonnaise

5 tablespoons (75 ml) sweetened condensed milk

¼ teaspoon rice vinegar

Neutral oil, such as canola, for frying

4 ounces (115 g) medium broccoli florets

1 pound (450 g) large shrimp, about 16 to 20, peeled and deveined

⅓ cup (40 g) cornstarch

1 teaspoon toasted sesame seeds

1. Prepare a sheet pan lined with parchment. In a small saucepan over medium heat, add 2 tablespoons of water, sugar, honey, and a pinch of salt. Stir occasionally to reduce slightly, 3 to 4 minutes. Add the walnuts to the saucepan; continue stirring the walnuts in the syrup until there is no liquid remaining and it completely coats the walnuts without dripping off. Transfer the walnuts to the prepared sheet pan, spreading them out to fully cool down.

2. In a small bowl, combine the mayonnaise, condensed milk, rice vinegar, and ¼ teaspoon salt, and stir until smooth. Season as needed and set aside.

3. Bring a medium pot of water to a boil; add the remaining salt and a splash of oil to the pot. Blanch the broccoli florets for 30 seconds, and immediately scoop them out to a clean bowl. Rinse them under cold water for 10 to 15 seconds; drain and set aside.

4. In a small saucepan, heat enough oil to reach about 3 inches (7 cm) on the side of the pot, over medium-high heat until it reaches 350°F (180°C). Dredge the shrimp in the cornstarch, shaking off any excess. Fry the shrimp in batches, gently stirring and flipping occasionally, until golden brown and cooked through, about 2 to 3 minutes per batch. Transfer the fried shrimp to a large mixing bowl. Pour the creamy sauce over the shrimp and gently toss until the shrimp are fully coated.

5. Arrange the shrimp, broccoli, and walnuts onto a serving plate, and sprinkle with the sesame seeds. Serve immediately.

Crispy Tofu *with* Scallion-Ginger Sauce

The key to crispy tofu isn't pressing all the water out of the slab or frying it in a lot of oil—it's coating the tofu in Kewpie Mayonnaise. Once these mayo-covered slices of tofu are slid into the oven, the oil in the condiment ends up frying the tofu, no eggy dredge or deep-fry needed. The tofu is crunchy on the outside, in part thanks to a panko-studded exterior, and squishy-in-a-good-way on the inside. This dish comes together in 20 minutes, making it a strong contender for a busy weeknight dinner—the tofu can be roasted alongside a tray of vegetables for a complete meal.

SERVES 2

- ¼ cup (25 g) finely minced scallions
- 3 tablespoons (40 g) finely minced ginger
- ⅓ cup (80 ml) toasted sesame oil
- 2 teaspoons salt, plus more as needed
- One 14-ounce (400 g) package firm tofu, drained and sliced ½-inch-thick (12 mm)
- 6 tablespoons (90 ml) Kewpie Mayonnaise
- 1 cup (100 g) panko bread crumbs

1. Preheat the oven to 425° F (220° C).
2. Make the scallion-ginger sauce: In a small bowl, combine the scallions, ginger, sesame oil, and ½ teaspoon salt. Mix thoroughly and season as needed.
3. Pat the tofu slices dry with paper towels.
4. In a small bowl, mix the mayonnaise with 1½ teaspoons salt. Brush to coat all sides of the tofu slices with the mayonnaise mixture, and then apply the rest of the mixture to the top of the tofu slices. Sprinkle the panko to cover the tops.
5. Place the tofu slices on a baking sheet with a fish spatula. Bake for 15 minutes, then broil on the top rack for 1 to 2 minutes, watching closely, until golden brown on top.
6. Carefully transfer the tofu to a serving plate and finish with the scallion-ginger sauce.

Karaage

Typically, this Japanese-style fried chicken is made by marinating chunks of chicken in soy sauce and sake, dredging them in starch, and then deep-frying them. This recipe calls for adding a bit of Kewpie Mayonnaise to that marinade, which prevents the meat from drying out and infuses it with flavor. Karaage is a popular main in bento boxes because it holds up well even after cooling. No matter what temperature you enjoy it at, karaage is best with a squeeze of lemon, a sprinkle of shichimi togarashi, and more Kewpie Mayonnaise on the side.

SERVES 2

- ¼ teaspoon kosher salt
- ½ teaspoon freshly ground black pepper
- ½ teaspoon grated ginger
- 2 teaspoons soy sauce
- 2 teaspoons sake
- 1 tablespoon Kewpie Mayonnaise, plus more for serving
- 1 pound (450 g) boneless, skinless chicken thighs, cut into 2-inch (5 cm) pieces
- 2 tablespoons potato starch or cornstarch, plus more as needed
- Neutral vegetable oil, such as canola, for frying
- Lemon wedges, for serving
- ½ teaspoon shichimi togarashi, for serving

1. In a medium bowl, whisk together the salt, black pepper, ginger, soy sauce, sake, and mayonnaise until combined. Add the chicken pieces, stirring to coat with the marinade. Cover and refrigerate for 30 minutes to 1 hour.

2. Lightly dredge each marinated chicken piece in the potato starch, shaking off excess starch. Repeat with the remaining chicken pieces.

3. In a heavy-bottomed pot, heat enough oil to reach about 3 inches (7 cm) on the side of the pot, over medium-high heat until it reaches 350°F (180°C).

4. Fry the chicken in batches, ensuring the oil temperature remains above 300°F (150°C). Fry for 4 to 5 minutes at 350°F (180°C), until crispy and golden brown. Transfer the fried chicken to a cooling rack and let it rest for 1 to 2 minutes.

5. Place the chicken on a serving plate alongside the extra mayonnaise and lemon wedges. The shichimi togarashi can be sprinkled over the chicken or served in a small dish on the side so eaters can control the spice level. The karaage will keep for up to 3 days in the fridge.

Hot Honey Baby Back Ribs

You don't need a grill or smoker to get sticky, tender baby back ribs. All you need is your trusty oven and some jazzed-up Kewpie Mayonnaise. The sweet and savory mayo marinade ensures that the ribs come out fall-off-the-bone soft and finger-licking delicious every time. If you're a heat seeker, feel free to up the cayenne in the marinade to make the ribs even spicier.

SERVES 4

- 3 pounds (1.36 kg) baby back ribs
- ½ cup (120 ml) Kewpie Mayonnaise
- 2 tablespoons packed brown sugar
- 2 tablespoons kosher salt
- 1 tablespoon garlic powder
- 1 teaspoon freshly ground black pepper
- ½ teaspoon paprika
- 1 tablespoon cayenne pepper
- ½ cup (120 ml) honey
- 1 teaspoon chili flakes
- 1 tablespoon soy sauce

1. If the backside of the ribs has a thin membrane over the bones, remove it by carefully sliding a knife under the membrane and then peeling it away. Line a baking sheet with aluminum foil.

2. In a small bowl stir together the mayonnaise, brown sugar, salt, garlic powder, black pepper, paprika, and cayenne pepper. Rub the mixture all over the ribs and place on the prepared baking sheet. Cover with foil and let the ribs marinate for 1 to 2 hours in the fridge.

3. Preheat the oven to 300°F (150°C). Bake the ribs until very tender, about 2 hours.

4. Make the hot honey: In a small bowl, combine the honey, chili flakes, and soy sauce and stir to mix well.

5. Turn oven to broil. Remove the foil from the ribs, put them on a clean baking sheet, and brush both sides with the hot honey. Broil until sauce just starts to caramelize, 2 to 4 minutes. Serve immediately on a platter or slice the ribs to desired serving portions.

デザート

desserts

JAPANESE FLUFFY PANCAKES 146

CHOCOLATE CAKE 150

CORNFLAKE COOKIES 153

LEMON CUPCAKES 156

APPLE GALETTE 158

Japanese Fluffy Pancakes

To get perfect Japanese pancakes—thick and wobbly—you need the right kind of leavening agents, a bit of technique, and some patience. That's a lot easier to pull off with two key ingredients in this recipe: egg whites whisked into meringue-like peaks and Kewpie Mayonnaise, which has emulsified oil and vinegar to help the batter rise (literally and figuratively) to the occasion. Make sure to follow the instructions for cooking the pancakes very carefully, because the unique method of layering the batter is crucial in achieving that height and cloud-like texture.

SERVES 1 (3 PANCAKES)

1 egg yolk

1 tablespoon Kewpie Mayonnaise

2½ tablespoons granulated sugar

¼ teaspoon kosher salt

2 tablespoons milk

3 tablespoons (23 g) all-purpose flour

¼ teaspoon baking powder

2 large egg whites

¼ teaspoon cornstarch

Neutral vegetable oil, such as canola, as needed

Powdered sugar, for serving

Butter, for serving

Whipped cream, for serving

Maple syrup, for serving

1. In a medium bowl, whisk the egg yolk and mayonnaise with 1 tablespoon granulated sugar and a pinch of salt until pale and frothy. Add the milk to the mixture in batches. Sift the flour and baking powder over the yolk mixture and whisk well, making sure everything is incorporated.

2. In a separate bowl, whip the egg whites until frothy and pale. Add the remaining granulated sugar gradually, then whisk in the cornstarch until the egg whites form a glossy, thick meringue that holds stiff peaks. Be careful not to overwhip.

3. Take ⅓ of the whipped egg whites and whisk it into the bowl with the yolk mixture until completely incorporated. Add half of the remaining whites and whisk, being careful not to deflate. Transfer the egg yolk mixture to the remaining egg whites, whisk, and then use a spatula to fold together.

4. Heat a large nonstick frying pan (with a lid) over low heat. Very lightly brush the pan with the oil and use a paper towel to spread the oil and coat the pan. Using an ice cream scoop or measuring cup, scoop three individual ¼ cups (30 g) of the batter onto the pan, leaving space in between. Cover and cook for 4 to 5 minutes.

5. Remove the lid and gently add ¼ cup (30 g) more batter on top of each pancake, trying to make it stay on top and not fall to the sides. It's important to let the pancake heat through for a few minutes before the additional scoop of batter; the steam gently cooks the pancake, so you get a fluffy interior and a barely crisp edge. Cover and continue to cook for 4 to 5 more minutes. Lift the lid and use a fish spatula to carefully peek under the pancake. The pancake should release easily—don't force it.

6. Gently flip. Cover and cook for 5 to 6 minutes. The pancakes will grow even taller and fluffier when they're done.

7. Once the pancakes are golden and cooked through, gently remove and serve on a plate with your preferred combination of powdered sugar, butter, whipped cream, and maple syrup. Enjoy right away.

KEWPIE IN THE WORLD

MAYONNAISE DAY

March 1 marks Kewpie Mayonnaise Day. Starting in 2016, the company christened this date as an unofficial holiday in Japan to honor the birth of Kewpie Mayonnaise in March 1925. For past Mayonnaise Days, Kewpie has created mayo-themed merch (shirts, keychains, even phone cases) and thrown various events for the public, such as monthlong mayonnaise pop-up cafés in Japan featuring dishes marinated, seasoned, and finished with the condiment. These events are so highly anticipated that they often get national and even international press coverage. For one recent café pop-up, some customers waited as long as 45 minutes to enter, which goes to show just how beloved Mayonnaise Day has become.

The calm before the storm at one of the ever popular Kewpie Mayonnaise pop-up cafés

IT'S A MAYOLER'S WORLD

These days, people define themselves by their astrological signs, sports team fealty, and coffee shop order. In Japan, another distinction divides folks into two categories: Are you or are you not a mayoler?

マヨラー, or "mayora" (Westernized to "mayoler"), is the Japanese term for people who love mayonnaise and put it on everything. Mayolers are a niche but somewhat influential group of people in Japan, sometimes referred to in anime and even given their own stickers on LINE, Japan's popular messaging app. At one point, there was even a restaurant in Tokyo made for mayolers; there customers could purchase their own bottle of mayonnaise to use and enjoy, like you would with a splurge-worthy whiskey at a high-end bar.

Kewpie doesn't endorse the mayoler lifestyle, however: "Too much consumption of one particular sauce or ingredient may not be good for the health in general," a representative says. Even so, one can't deny that mayolers are proof that Nakashima's goal of bringing mayonnaise into the very center of Japanese culture has been achieved.

Chocolate Cake

Mayonnaise was a common ingredient in Depression-era American recipes for chocolate cake, where it was used as a substitute for eggs and butter when those ingredients were scarce. Still today, some bakers swear by mayonnaise as the secret ingredient to a moist texture and an extra-soft crumb. This recipe builds on the storied tradition of a mayo-spiked batter but also adds a few tablespoons of brewed coffee. It doesn't need to be hot, but make sure the coffee is freshly brewed for it to really intensify the chocolaty flavor. A single layer of the cake is excellent when dusted with powdered sugar, but this recipe can also be doubled or tripled to create a layer cake that is finished with a frosting of your choosing.

MAKES 1 9-INCH CAKE

Baking spray, as needed

2 cups (240 g) all-purpose flour, sifted

1 cup (200 g) granulated sugar

½ teaspoon kosher salt

⅓ cup (30 g) unsweetened baking cocoa

2 teaspoons baking soda

1 cup (240 ml) Kewpie Mayonnaise

1 teaspoon vanilla extract

3 tablespoons (45 ml) black coffee

1 tablespoon powdered sugar

1. Preheat the oven to 350°F (180°C). Spray a 9-inch (23 cm) round cake pan with baking spray.

2. In a large bowl, mix together the flour, granulated sugar, salt, baking cocoa, and baking soda. In a separate bowl, whisk together 1 cup (240 ml) of water, mayonnaise, vanilla extract, and coffee.

3. Slowly add the liquid mixture into the dry ingredients. Stir just until combined. Pour into the prepared pan.

4. Bake for about 35 to 40 minutes, until a toothpick inserted comes out clean. Dust with the powdered sugar or spread with your favorite frosting.

5. Store in an airtight container at room temperature for up to 4 days, or wrap in plastic wrap and keep in the refrigerator up to a week—just let sit at room temperature for 30 minutes before serving.

Cornflake Cookies

When the craving for something sweet hits but the pantry and fridge are looking bleak, this seven-ingredient cookie is there for you. It relies entirely on cupboard staples—sugar, flour, salt, vanilla extract—and it doesn't need eggs or even oil, thanks to Kewpie Mayonnaise, which already has all of that. The process is just as easy: Dump everything in a bowl, mix, scoop into balls, and bake. If you're low on cereal, you can do without the cornflakes and enjoy the simple bliss of this crisp, toasty vanilla cookie.

MAKES 10 COOKIES
---

1 cup (200 grams) granulated sugar

2 cups (240 grams) all-purpose flour

1 teaspoon baking soda

¼ teaspoon kosher salt

1 cup (240 ml) Kewpie Mayonnaise

1 teaspoon vanilla extract

½ cup (14 g) cornflake cereal

1. Preheat the oven to 350°F (180°C) and line a baking sheet with parchment paper.
2. In a large mixing bowl, combine the sugar, flour, baking soda, and salt.
3. In a small bowl, mix together the mayonnaise and vanilla extract until well incorporated.
4. Add the mayonnaise mixture to the dry ingredients, stirring with a spatula until well blended.
5. Shape the dough into walnut-sized balls, about 1 ounce (30 g) each, and place them on the prepared baking sheet, leaving a 1-inch space between each cookie. Gently flatten each ball with your fingers or a small offset spatula.
6. Sprinkle the cornflakes on top of each cookie, pressing lightly to adhere.
7. Bake for 12 minutes, or until the edges are golden.
8. Allow the cookies to cool completely on the baking sheet for 15 to 20 minutes before serving. Store at room temperature, out of direct sunlight, in an airtight container for up to a week.

The
PEOPLE BEHIND KEWPIE MAYO

RURIKO YAMAGUCHI

CURRENT ROLE AT KEWPIE CORPORATION:
Tour communicator at Mayoterrace, Kewpie Mayonnaise's mayo museum in Tokyo

Why did you want to work at the company?
"I joined Kewpie because I love both Kewpie dolls and Kewpie Mayonnaise," Yamaguchi says. She started at one of Kewpie's manufacturing factories, operating the egg-cracking machine before moving into managing museum tours.

How did you get into leading tours?
"On my first day, a melody signaling visitors started playing in the factory, so I wondered what it was and looked up, and saw children looking at us through the window. It was an elementary school field trip," she remembers. "I immediately thought, 'I want to do that job!'" That same day, Yamaguchi asked her boss to be transferred to the tour department. However, tour communicators needed on-the-ground experience, she was told, and after three years, she was ready.

What's the most surprising thing you've learned about Kewpie Mayonnaise?
"Mayonnaise hacks!" Yamaguchi shares. She uses the condiment for fluffier pancakes, juicier hamburgers, and shrimp tempura, no egg dip or bread crumbs needed. "I use the mayonnaise as the batter," Yamaguchi explains. "It can be fried crisply and deliciously with just mayonnaise, flour, and water."

What do you love about your job?
"I love seeing visitors enjoy the tour, feeling as inspired as I am not only by the mayonnaise but also Kewpie's philosophy, passion, and effort in the manufacturing processes," she says. Yamaguchi also enjoys answering any questions visitors have. One consistent ask is: How do you use up all the mayonnaise in the bottle? She suggests shaking it up with other ingredients to make a dressing (page 64).

KEWPIE IN THE WORLD

MAYOTERRACE

True fans make their pilgrimage to Mayoterrace, a museum in Tokyo dedicated to Kewpie Mayonnaise. In 1961, local elementary students asked to tour the Kewpie factories, to which the company happily agreed, and in 2014, an entire museum was created just for visitors. Kewpie transformed an old production plant into Mayoterrace, complete with a room shaped like the iconic Kewpie bottle. Enthusiastic guides donning brightly hued berets lead visitors through the history of the company, the process behind making the mayonnaise (including, for example, the air shower used to remove any debris from employees), and a hands-on cooking demo. There is no script for tour leaders; rather, each guide goes off their own experience and the energy and desires of the tour group. Admission is free to the public, and nearly 100,000 visitors come each year to get an inside look into how the sausage, er, mayonnaise is made.

Naturally, the entrance to the Kewpie-bottle-shaped room at Mayoterrace is through the red cap.

Lemon Cupcakes

Serious bakers know that vinegar can help create an airy crumb, and Kewpie Mayonnaise has quite a bit of it. It lightens this decadent batter enriched with butter and milk, resulting in a fluffier texture with an ever-so-slight tang. This recipe leans into that tanginess by grating lemon zest directly into the batter. The classic vanilla frosting balances all the citrusy and milky flavors—it's the literal icing on the (cup)cake.

MAKES 12 CUPCAKES

FOR THE CUPCAKES

- 1⅓ cups (165 g) all-purpose flour
- 1½ teaspoons baking powder
- ¼ teaspoon kosher salt
- ½ cup (114 g) unsalted butter, melted and cooled
- 2 tablespoons lemon zest
- 1 cup (200 g) granulated sugar
- 1 large egg
- ¼ cup (60 ml) Kewpie Mayonnaise
- ½ cup (120 ml) cold milk or buttermilk
- 6 tablespoons (90 ml) lemon juice

FOR THE FROSTING

- ¾ cup (170 g) unsalted butter, room temperature
- ¼ teaspoon kosher salt
- 1 teaspoon vanilla extract
- 3 cups (375 g) powdered sugar
- 3 tablespoons (45 ml) cream or milk
- Sliced lemons, for serving (optional)

1. Preheat the oven to 350°F (180°C) and line a muffin pan with 12 paper liners.

2. Make the cupcake batter: Mix the flour, baking powder, and salt with a fork in a large bowl.

3. In a medium bowl, whisk together the melted butter, lemon zest, and granulated sugar. Then mix in the egg, mayonnaise, cold milk, and lemon juice.

4. Add the wet ingredients to the dry ingredients. Whisk until just smooth and combined. Divide the batter into the 12 cupcake liners.

5. Bake for about 20 to 22 minutes or until a toothpick inserted into the center comes out clean. Let cool completely before frosting.

6. Make the frosting: Use a stand mixer with a paddle attachment or handheld mixer to beat the room-temperature butter, salt, and vanilla extract until light and fluffy.

7. Add the powdered sugar to the butter mixture, 1 cup (125 g) at a time, mixing well in between. Add in the cream, 1 tablespoon at a time as needed, until the frosting has no dry clumps and becomes smooth and spreadable.

8. Beat on high speed for about 1 minute after the last addition of powdered sugar for a fluffy and airy texture. Frost the cupcakes as desired, and garnish with lemon slices, if using.

9. If making ahead of time, store the unfrosted cupcakes in an airtight container at room temperature for up to 4 days, or wrapped in plastic and kept in the refrigerator up to a week. Leave at room temperature for 30 minutes before frosting and serving.

Apple Galette

A galette is essentially pie without the fuss—no blind baking, no latticework. This apple galette is made even easier by the five-ingredient dough, which relies on Kewpie Mayonnaise. This one ingredient creates a tender, buttery crust sans tediously forming chunks of butter with a pastry cutter or endlessly folding and forming the dough to get all those layers. The galette dough comes together in a flash and can easily be loaded with the macerated apple slices for a baked good that's as impressive as it is easy. This versatile dough can also be used for savory galettes as well as quiche and, yes, even pies.

SERVES 2 TO 4

FOR THE DOUGH

- 1½ cups (180 g) all-purpose flour, sifted, plus more for dusting
- ¾ teaspoon granulated sugar
- ½ teaspoon kosher salt
- ¼ teaspoon baking powder
- 6 tablespoons (90 ml) Kewpie Mayonnaise
- 2 to 5 teaspoons ice-cold water

1. Make the galette dough: Mix the flour, granulated sugar, salt, and baking powder together in a large bowl. Add the mayonnaise and mix with a fork until it resembles coarse sand. Gradually add the ice-cold water, 1 teaspoon at a time, and mix with your hands until a doughball forms. Shape the dough into a disk, wrap it in plastic, and refrigerate for at least 1 hour.

2. Make the filling: Gently toss the apples, brown sugar, lemon juice, cornstarch, cinnamon, ginger, fine salt, and vanilla extract together in a large bowl.

3. Line a rimmed sheet pan with parchment paper.

FOR THE FILLING

- 1 pound tart apples such as Granny Smith, Jonagold, Honeycrisp, Braeburn, or Mutsu (about 2 to 4 apples), peeled and cut into ¼-inch-thick (6 mm) slices
- ¼ cup (50 g) lightly packed light brown sugar
- 1 tablespoon lemon juice
- 2 teaspoons cornstarch
- ½ teaspoon ground cinnamon
- ½ teaspoon ground ginger
- ⅛ teaspoon fine salt
- ½ teaspoon vanilla extract
- 1 large egg
- Coarse sugar
- 1 tablespoon yuzu or apricot jam

4. Remove the chilled dough from the refrigerator and let it sit at room temperature for 5 to 10 minutes or until pliable. On a lightly floured counter, roll the dough into a 13-inch (33 cm) circle, then transfer it to the prepared pan.

5. Using a slotted spoon, pick up the apples from the bowl, leaving the excess juice behind, and arrange them in the center of the dough, leaving a 2-inch (5 cm) border around the edge. Carefully grasp one edge of the dough and fold it up 2 inches (5 cm) over the apples. Repeat around the circumference of the tart, overlapping the dough every 2 inches (5 cm). Gently pinch the pleated dough to secure, but do not press the dough into the fruit.

6. Place in the fridge to chill while you preheat the oven. Adjust the oven rack to the lower-middle position and heat the oven to 375°F (190°C).

7. While preheating, beat the egg with ½ teaspoon of water. Brush all over the unbaked crust. Sprinkle the crust with coarse sugar. Bake the galette until the crust is deep golden brown and the fruit is bubbling, 50 minutes to 1 hour.

8. Using two spatulas, carefully transfer the galette (still on the parchment) to a wire rack and let cool for 10 minutes.

9. While the galette cools, combine the yuzu jam and 1 teaspoon of water in a small glass bowl. Microwave for 15 to 20 seconds or until bubbling. Brush over the apples.

10. Loosen the tart from the parchment and carefully slide it onto a wire rack using two spatulas; let cool until warm, about 30 minutes. Cut into wedges and serve.

11. If serving later, store in an airtight container at room temperature for up to 2 days or in the fridge for up to a week.

KEWPIE BY THE DECADE

The 2010s & 2020s

As Kewpie solidified its American presence (read more on page 5), the company decided to expand in Asia as well. Kewpie set up shop in China, Thailand, Malaysia, Vietnam, and Indonesia, building manufacturing facilities, hiring local employees, and closely observing how new customers responded to its products. The latter led to some crafty innovation that would have gotten the approval of Nakashima, Kewpie's founder.

For example, in China, Kewpie noticed how locals, both chefs and home cooks, used mayonnaise in fruit salads, as opposed to drizzling it on raw vegetables and in green salads. So the company introduced a sweetened version of Kewpie Mayonnaise to complement fruit and bread. This product has turned out to be the preferred mayonnaise among Chinese customers. And to meet the needs of diners in Malaysia, which has a large Muslim population, local employees helped Kewpie Mayonnaise earn a halal certification. In all these regions, Kewpie was largely unknown despite its geographic proximity. Employees had to visit bakeries and restaurants in person to introduce the product, just as Nakashima and his team did in the early days of Kewpie Mayonnaise.

Back on home soil in Japan, Kewpie celebrated each new decade—and in a very Kewpie way. The company hosted a cooking competition delightfully dubbed the Mayo 1 Grand Prix, created an account on LINE (Japan's go-to messaging app), and published an internal company cookbook with recipes from employees. But that's just a precursor to the big event.

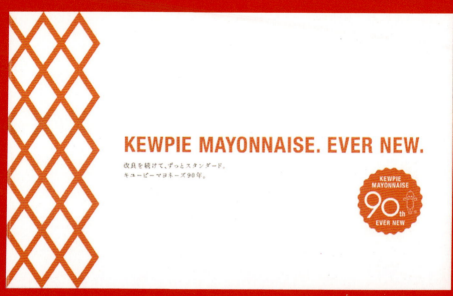

To commemorate its 90th anniversary, Kewpie Mayonnaise published its own book, complete with notes from employees.

KEWPIE KEEPS GOING

In 2025, Kewpie Mayonnaise commemorated its one hundredth anniversary with this very cookbook (and fittingly, another mayonnaise factory in America). Throughout its history—from the hardship of war and its repercussions, to a growing and heated mayonnaise competition in Japan, to the shift in markets due to globalization and social media—Kewpie has been spreading its creamy richness and quirky ways. That Kewpie can celebrate one hundred years of existence is not only proof of the universal love for the condiment, but a testament to the legacy of Nakashima and his cherished Japanese-style mayonnaise.

It's not a celebration without a logo. "Ever New" speaks to Kewpie's desire to continually improve.

Kewpie employees (and the character in a chef's toque) offering a taste of mayonnaise to shoppers in Indonesia

INDEX

A
apple galette, 158–159
avocado tuna salad, 68

B
bottle anatomy, Kewpie Mayonnaise, 14–15, 61
burgers
    cheeseburgers, 129
    shrimp, 122–123

C
Caesar salad, 62–63
cake, chocolate, 150–151
California roll, 86–87
carbonara, 102–103
cauliflower, Buffalo cauliflower bites, 44
cheese
    cheeseburgers, 129
    grilled cheese sandwich, 120–121
    mac and, 110–111
    pimento dip, 28–29
chicken
    karaage, 140–141
    soy-glazed chicken wings, 36–37
chocolate cake, 150–151
classes on mayonnaise, 128
coleslaw, 66–67
cookies, cornflake, 152–153

corn
    cornflake cookies, 152–153
    dip, 26–27
    shichimi grilled, 48–49
creamy mashed potatoes, 54–55
crudité, 24–25
cupcakes, lemon, 156–157

D
dip
    corn, 26–27
    crudité, 24–25
    formula, 32
    pimento cheese, 28–29
    smoked fish, 30–31
dressing, ranch, 24–25

E
eggs
    deviled, 20–21
    egg fried rice, 90

F
fish
    fish roe udon, 92–93
    fish taco, 132–133
    smoked fish dip, 30–31
    See also salmon; seafood; tuna
formula of Kewpie Mayonnaise, 12–13

fries, seaweed, 42–43
fritto misto, 134–135

G

garlic
    garlic mayonnaise tomato sandwich, 58–59
    garlic roasted potatoes, 52–53
green goddess potato salad, 72–73
grilled cheese sandwich, 120–121

H

history, Kewpie, 3–6
    1920s, 22–23
    1930s, 34–35
    1940s, 50–51
    1950s, 56–57
    1960s, 74–75
    1970s, 82–83
    1980s, 96–97
    1990s, 114–115
    2000s, 114–115
    2010s, 160–161
    2020s, 160–161
honey-walnut shrimp, 136–137
hot honey baby back ribs, 142–143

J

Japanese fluffy pancakes, 146–147
Japanese potato salad, 70–71

K

karaage, 140–141
katsu sando, 117, 119
Kewpie character, 7
Kobayashi, Hideaki, 33

L

lemon cupcakes, 156–157

M

mac and cheese, 110–111
mayolers, 149
Mayonnaise Day, 148
Mayo Terrace, 155
meatballs, spaghetti and, 108–109
Mori, Yoshimitsu, 94
Mothers' Chorus Festival, 69
music, 45

N

Nakashima, Toichiro, 8–9, 10–11
noodles
    fish roe udon, 92–93
    instantly creamy ramen, 98–99
    yakisoba, 100–101

O

okonomiyaki, 130–131

P

pancakes
    Japanese fluffy, 146–147
    okonomiyaki, 130–131
pasta
    carbonara, 102–103
    mac and cheese, 110–111
    spaghetti and meatballs, 108–109
pie, apple galette, 158–159
pimento cheese dip, 28–29
plate patterns, 60
potatoes
    creamy mashed, 54–55
    garlic roasted, 52–53

green goddess potato salad, 72–73
Japanese potato salad, 70–71
takoyaki, 38–39
products, Kewpie, 104–107

R

ramen, instantly creamy, 98–99
ranch dressing, 24–25
recipe enhancements with Kewpie Mayonnaise, 91
ribs, hot honey baby back, 142–143
rice
    California roll, 86–87
    egg fried, 90
    sesame salmon onigiri, 78–79
    spicy tuna rice bowl, 84–85
    sushi bake, 88–89

S

salad
    avocado tuna, 68
    Caesar, 62–63
    coleslaw, 66–67
    green goddess potato, 72–73
    Japanese potato, 70–71
    sesame wedge, 64–65
salmon
    sesame salmon onigiri, 78–79
    torched salmon don, 80–81
sandwich
    grilled cheese, 120–121
    katsu sando, 117, 119
    tamago, 116, 118
    tomato with garlic mayonnaise, 58–59
sauce
    scallion-ginger, 138–139
    tartar, 134–135

seafood, fritto misto, 134–135
    See also fish; salmon; seaweed; shrimp; tuna
seaweed fries, 42–43
sesame salmon onigiri, 78–79
sesame wedge salad, 64–65
shichimi grilled corn, 48–49
shrimp
    burgers, 122–123
    honey-walnut, 136–137
    oven-fried, 40–41
soy-glazed chicken wings, 36–37
spaghetti and meatballs, 108–109
spicy tuna rice bowl, 84–85
sushi
    California roll, 86–87
    sushi bake, 88–89

T

taco, fish, 132–133
takoyaki, potato, 38–39
tamago sando, 116, 118
tamagoyaki, 18–19
tartar sauce, 134–135
three-minute cooking, 95
tofu, crispy, 138–139
tomato sandwich and garlic mayonnaise, 58–59
tuna
    and avocado salad, 68
    spicy tuna rice bowl, 84–85

W

worldwide spread of Kewpie Mayonnaise, 124–127

Y

yakisoba, 100–101
Yamaguchi, Ruriko, 154

ACKNOWLEDGMENTS

Celebrating one hundred years of Kewpie Mayonnaise—and in cookbook form—has been a big and exciting undertaking.

Kewpie Corporation would like to thank Ms. Ayako Osawa and Ms. Akiko Tamura, based at the Tokyo headquarters, for their insight, help, and enthusiasm in making this cookbook happen.

—**KEWPIE CORPORATION**

This cookbook has been an absolute delight to work on, and this is due to so many people. Thank you to my agent, Danielle Svetcov, for asking me if I wanted to work on a Kewpie Mayonnaise cookbook (you know me!) as well as your invaluable guidance throughout the process, and to my fellow collaborators Jessie, Eugene, and Heami for making each step so fun. Thank you to my editors Bella Lemos and Judy Pray for your smart and thoughtful edits and to the team at Workman for making this cookbook look so good. Thank you to my parents Brian and Debi Inamine for your love and support over the years and to my husband Travis Wong for reading everything I write and dreaming big with me. And finally, thank you to everyone at Kewpie Corporation for trusting me with telling this incredible story (and taking time to hop on late-night Zoom calls).

—**ELYSE INAMINE**

We made a Kewpie book! It's a dream come true to write for a brand I love. I'm endlessly grateful to my brilliant coauthor, Elyse Inamine, for your trust and insight, and to Danielle Svetcov for your guidance. Thank you to Bella Lemos, Judy Pray, and the Workman Publishing team for your sharp eyes and support. Nicole Wang, your proposal design and tremendous help on recipe testing. Eugene Ho, Heami Lee, and Julia Rose, your work makes the recipes absolutely stunning. To Kewpie lovers, my readers, and supporters—your enthusiasm makes writing and developing recipes meaningful and worthwhile.

—**JESSIE YUCHEN**

ABOUT THE AUTHOR

Kewpie Corporation was founded in 1919 by Toichiro Nakashima, whose aspiration was to "contribute to the health of the Japanese people." In 1925, Nakashima created Kewpie Mayonnaise, which is one of the most popular condiments in Japan today. In addition to its beloved mayonnaise, Kewpie Corporation creates a variety of products including salad dressings, fruit jams, and pasta sauces that are sold across the world. Kewpie Corporation is based in Shibuya, Tokyo.